CARLY BUTLER

M000288638

ONE WOMAN'S JOURNEY RETRACING
THE STEPS OF HER GRANDMOTHER'S
LOVE LETTERS, 67 YEARS LATER

www.lifesletter.com

Copyright © 2021 by Carly Butler Verheyen.

All rights reserved. No part of this publication may be reproduced, distributed, or transmitted in any form or by any means, including photocopying, recording, or other electronic or mechanical methods, without the prior written permission of the publisher, except in the case of brief quotations embodied in critical reviews and certain other noncommercial uses permitted by copyright law. For permission requests, write to the author at:

Carly Butler Verheyen
lifesletter.com
lifesletter@gmail.com

Life's Letter – Carly Butler Verheyen — 1st ed.
ISBN Paperback B&W: 978-1-7777679-1-4
Hardcover colour: 978-1-7777679-0-7

Carly Butler Verheyen would like to acknowledge the support of the Ontario Arts Council.

ONTARIO ARTS COUNCIL
CONSEIL DES ARTS DE L'ONTARIO

an Ontario government agency
un organisme du gouvernement de l'Ontario

To my family.
Past, present, & future.
May the life stories & love letters
of your heart continue being told.

Note from the author

This memoir has been written to the best of my memory using journals, letters, conversations, and photographs. My blog posts from my time in England inspired some of the content in this book, so some of you may recognize things here and there. Some names and identifying characteristics have been changed, but not all.

TABLE OF CONTENTS

PRAISE FOR LIFE'S LETTER

"Finding 100 love letters of her grandmother's set Carly Verheyen on a journey of discovery that will open up your eyes, make you see not only a little of the soul of this war bride who fell in love with a Canadian soldier, but a little more about the granddaughter who wanted to know more, and to tell more. The letters nearly were tossed out when the family was sorting through the family home, but once they were found, Verheyen set out to walk in her grandmother's life, to find out what she did on an ordinary day in Britain, the house she lived in, the places she shopped. In some ways, Carly Verheyen was prepared for this. Having worked in the banking industry, and helping heartbroken widows and family members sort through their sudden loss, she proved to be a good listener, someone who paid attention to the emotional and personal moments that define us all. In this book, you will see her navigate through the words of her grandmother as she sketches a story that is as much her grandmother's as it is a story about a whole generation that defined the future for those to follow. It is a perceptive, moving, and wonderful book that you won't want to put down once you start in."

MARTY GERVAIS, author of the bestselling book
The Rumrunners

"Life's Letter was a wonderful read and offers such a unique and captivating way to explore one's lineage. The love letters transport the reader to another time and place with love and adventure as the main characters throughout. This book serves as a reminder of just how much our past can inform our present."

LAUREN ELLMAN, author of *BRB: A Memoir About Coming of Age in the Digital Age*

"An incredible odyssey beautifully told."

JANICE MACLEOD, New York Times best selling author of
Paris Letters

"This book will take you back in time to retrace the paths of two people falling further in love by way of letter writing. But the story only begins there... Through piecing together the story of her grandparents, Carly dares to step into a life she truly loves-- one that is uncommon, messy, beautiful, and entirely hers. This book is a love letter to every person who picks it up-- a fierce reminder to wake up and live your best life now. There is no time to waste and only you can approach the things that make your heart beat wildly."

HANNAH BRENCHER, author of *Fighting Forward* and *Come Matter Here*

CHAPTER I

FROM BEHIND THE WICKET

I knew I wasn't a lifer pretty early on in my career at the bank, but it became even clearer when I started to do some soul searching upon returning home from an adventure abroad teaching English in South Korea. My job at the bank was comfortable and it was my constant. Everything else seemed to change around me – boyfriends, the destination of my next trip, and the cities that I decided to live in. The bank was always there, like a loyal companion that was loving, supportive, and always welcoming me back with open arms. This time felt different though. I knew there had to be something more.

My favourite part of the job was meeting such interesting people from all walks of life with fascinating life stories. At one point around this time, I considered starting a blog called From Behind The Wicket, but confidentiality concerns kyboshed that idea. At one point, I made it my daily goal to dig into at least one life story per shift. I was mining for life story gold. Forget sales goals, I didn't care about the metrics of my job, but I did care about that warm, fuzzy feeling that I got when I saw someone shift into that moment when they became cracked open by the friendly teller who was handing them their 20s and was sharing a story that they may not have told in a long time.

There was the family that had been in Canada from Iraq for only a few days, spoke very little English, and wound up at my wicket with a translator. I looked them in the eyes with such curiosity and compassion and welcomed them to Canada as I counted them their colourful Canadian cash for the first time. They were bombed in a church in Iraq, had to seek medical care in an Italian hospital, and arrived in Windsor, Ontario for brand new lives as refugees. In that moment, I realized that these people had seen more horror and fear and displacement than I would ever know.

Then, there was the Filipino woman who had been in Canada for six years building a life for her family, including the 7-, 8-, and 10-year-old children she left behind as babies. She was absolutely beside herself with emotion at my wicket because the next day she was going to the airport to pick up her children. She had only seen them online for the past six years. I was in awe and really saw her in that moment and celebrated the excitement that she must have been feeling to finally be together again at last. I told her to bring them in to meet me once they got settled, and in they walked a few weeks later as a happy family together again.

The day I met the Holocaust survivor Lola, who soon became my 80-year-old bestie, is one that I'll never forget. It was October of 2010 and she had brought in a cheque from Germany. As I enquired about the cheque and deposited it into her account, she looked up at me with a story in her eyes, saying, "Yes, these are regular cheques I receive, I'm a Holocaust survivor, and I worked for them in concentration camps, and they pay me for life."

My family had just recently connected with some extended family members and had plans to attend my second cousin's Bat Mitzvah in New York. It was right before we were about to leave for the trip that I met Lola. I immediately connected with her about this and told her about us going on this family trip. When she heard that it was a relative that I was going to celebrate, her eyes lit up and she asked if I was Jewish. I told her about how my mother's mom was Jewish, and she declared on the spot that I was, in fact, Jewish.

She went on to tell me stories of what it was like for her going through the war during the Holocaust. She told me about the day that she was separated and taken from her family home and how that was the last time that she ever saw her family. She shared the story of the chance meeting of her husband after the war as they were fleeing in trains after liberation and how they moved to Canada and what their life was like as new Canadians in the 40s. She would tell me these stories over tea, when I would go to visit at her apartment overlooking the Detroit River.

Something happened when I started to pay attention to these bigger things that were going on around me at my day job. I would get goosebumps and know that this was what I was supposed to follow. I'm sure that a love for life stories was always there for me in subtle ways, but I just wasn't as aware of it until this time in my life. I started paying attention in new ways.

I was listening to more than just their words. I was curious. I could see in peoples' expressions, the way their eyes would light up or their response, that they felt something while sharing these stories with me. It was like I was in the conversation, but also witnessing people at the same time. I was seeing how it was impacting the person to be asked, and I was just there listening, witnessing and holding the space for them to share. I would ask a simple question, and people would open up to me. You could tell in their eyes that they hadn't been asked this question in a long time, if ever.

That was when I thought to myself that something was happening here. I was different from the people that were standing next to me. This was part of my power or gift that I bring to the world. I create the space or open up the conversation in this way that makes people feel safe and want to tell me their stories.

The handwritten piece that really spoke to me was the woman who came in a few days after her mother had passed away, the grief and sadness written all over her face. I was with her in that moment, and I was helping her get the documents ready to deal with her mother's estate. When I brought over the original signature card that her mother had signed when she originally opened the account, her eyes welled up with tears as she ran her fingers across her mother's handwritten signature. She whispered under her breath, "That's my mom."

It was in that moment that I thought back to my grandmother's cursive in those 110 love letters that we stumbled upon a few years back. The cursive, the letters, the family documents, and the family stories were all little signs that were leading me back to the letters.

CHAPTER 2

THE LOVE LETTERS

I n August of 2009, my mother packed up and moved my 87-year-old Papa Nick into an assisted living home. Since the death of my grandmother Rene 11 years prior, we all began to notice that the home in which they lived for most of their married life was simply far too big. His health was declining and he needed assistance almost daily. Even taking the amount of pills he was prescribed was taxing.

It took almost a week for my mom to work through the life her parents had built together. She sifted through a houseful of memories and went through their belongings room by room. The plan was to pack his essentials into the van and sort the rest into boxes that would be sold at the in-house auction the following week before putting the house on the market.

At the end of each day, my mom called me exhausted. She recounted the finds she had made that day – the scrapbook Grama had brought with her from England six decades earlier, precious family photos she had forgotten about, beautiful tea sets, and treasured jewelry Grama wore every day. Every night when we talked, Mom seemed buoyed by the life her parents had led. Seeing all the reminders of how happy they had been gave her the strength to get up the next day and plow through another roomful of memories.

On the last day, I was surprised to hear excitement rather than exhaustion in her voice. She had spent the day in my grandfather's tiny den where he watched sports from his man throne, a La-Z-Boy recliner from the 1980s.

She was going through the cupboards and bookshelves and was sorting VHS tapes that my grandfather hadn't had the heart to get rid of. Old family videos, British soap operas Grama had recorded, and any sort of news coverage of the Queen and Royal Family that Grama always watched with pride. As my mom was moving a stack of VHS tapes into a box, she noticed a plastic Big V pharmacy bag that was full of papers wedged in the back corner. Who knows how many of these bags she had been through that week. Grama loved squirreling things away. Hotel shampoo bottles and tiny, travel-size soaps from their trips, unused coupons clipped from decades of newspapers, and the endless souvenirs she picked up from every adventure they went on. Every time she opened a drawer or a cabinet and found a bag of Grama's treasures, she missed her more.

When she pulled the plastic bag out, she tossed it into the trash pile. It was as if she didn't have the heart to go through another one, but something made her stop. She reached for it and expected it to be just another bag of unused yarn, scraps of material Grama thought might come in handy, or a collection of birthday and holiday cards. She prayed this was the last one she would have to go through.

As she pulled the papers out of the plastic bag, she immediately realized that they were more than just papers. They were love letters. Over 100 fragile airmail letters scripted with love from her mom to her dad. At first glance, they looked like they were postmarked from 1946, just after the war. They were addressed to my grandfather in Canada with a return address of my grandmother's home in England. She figured they must have been from when they were apart before Grama moved to Canada as a war bride. She sat and stared at them in disbelief.

Grama had told my mom about these letters, but she was sure they had been lost or destroyed. Papa told her so many times about how he had burned the letters he had written to Grama when they were waiting for her to come to Canada. When she asked him why, he said, "That was a long time ago and that stuff was personal." But somehow Grama's letters to *him* survived.

As she flipped through the stack, she called me to tell me what she had discovered. I could hear in her voice how thrilled she was. She had little to connect her to that time in her parents' lives before she and her brother Roger were born. She had the stories they told about how they met and about their wedding. She knew they were separated for six months while Grama, a British war bride, waited for her travel papers so she could join her Canadian soldier husband in her new home. But until that day all she had were stories.

Papa had gotten rid of anything that reminded him of his time in the Army. He donated his uniform to the local legion and wartime museums and gave his metals and other memorabilia to my brother Ryan. He didn't want to hold on to anything from that time, especially the memories. He always said that the only good thing that happened to him during the war was meeting Grama. He didn't want to relive it. He didn't even watch movies about the war. It wasn't until he was in his 90s that he started talking more about it. Not until after my grandmother passed away did he agree to give an interview for Pier 21, the Canadian Museum of Immigration in Halifax.

Papa as a soldier

INTERVIEWER: What do you remember about that day the war was declared in 1939?

PAPA: *I was working with this man on a tobacco farm. We had a load of tobacco and were just going to hang it in the barn. He had three sons my age and he said, "I'm going in the house for a drink." He came running out of the house saying, "They've done it! They've done it!" I said, "They've done what?" He said, "They declared war, what are we gonna do?" I said, "If we don't get the tobacco in the barn, we're gonna be here til midnight." I was not worried, but he was so worried about his sons. In 1939 I was 17 and I figured I still had some time and probably by the time I reach the age, why, it'd be over. But I was wrong. Very wrong. Then in December of 1941 when we turned the radio on and the Japanese bombed Pearl Harbour, when the Americans declared war, well I tell ya, I thought when they get in there they'd surely end it in a hurry. Wrong again. I enlisted on September the 13th, 1942. I went to do my basic in Dundurn, Saskatchewan. I was there for almost a year then my unit moved on to Camp Borden in Ontario.*

A really peculiar thing happened there. We were under canvas and orders came down that we were all supposed to go up to the hall there and sign for new blankets. You were to take your old blankets in and sign for new blankets. So we went up there to get our new blankets, and I think they just gave us the same blankets back after we signed and they said, "Everybody wait out there until we're finished." So we all waited outside and then our Colonel came out and said, "Now do you fellas know what ya signed for?" "Blankets!" "No. You didn't. You signed to go overseas." And I thought that was really small of the army to do such a thing, to cheat ya. They cheated us into signing that, you know.

INTERVIEWER: **They actually staged it and it was actually your overseas forms?**

PAPA: *That's right. You should have seen the boys going over the hill that night. Two went over the hill and they sent the squad to go pick em up, bring 'em back, put two guards on them, turn around then four more would be gone. We must have had 20 people go over in the ridge.*

INTERVIEWER: **I can't believe they did that.**

PAPA: *Me neither, because they volunteered for active service. And if they would have put it as an honest question, they probably wouldn't have had a single problem with our unit either. I was not happy with that deal at all. But I mean hey, I figured it was just another way, another game.*

In July, we took the train to Windsor, Nova Scotia and were under canvas there for three days before we boarded the Queen Elizabeth in Halifax. It was quite a trip, we got over there in four days and five nights. We went 1000 miles out of way up by Iceland, and changed course every seven minutes. They told us, "If you go overboard, don't bother hollering for help, cause we're not stopping."

Papa under canvas

INTERVIEWER: **What port did you come into in England?**

PAPA: *We docked on the Firth of Forth in Scotland and they took us off in jetty's and we boarded a train there and then we went straight through to Woking in England. It's an army camp there, and a big castle. They had a lot of spider opts there, too. So that's what we were in, we got in around midnight. Still operating as a unit. We left Woking (after 3 weeks) and then to Red Hill (2 weeks) then Headley Downs and we were there for a good 6 months. Then they came along and said, "Okay, turn in your rifles, you're going to work." So we had to go to work in a factory there in Camp Worden, England putting vehicles together. See our unit was mostly from the Windsor area, so a lot of the guys work for GM, Chrysler and Ford. Worked on the line before, so they figured they might as well utilize the experience. So we were down putting vehicles together. It was a good life. We were doing that for about 6 months. And then when we got all of the vehicles together, we had a big supply of them. Then they came along one day, called a big parade and the colonel came out and said, "Gentlemen, I've got some bad news for you. Our unit has been disbanded. They don't need any more reccy outfits. We're taking you back to Woking." And we were in the big square in Woking and it was like a horseshoe. I was over here in this corner and this major got up there and he said, "Gentlemen, we need 300 volunteers for the tanks! If you want to go to the tanks, take one pace forward." And I think I was the first one up. And then of course they started going. Then they got more than 300. So then he said, "Okay, we started over there, so we'll count from over there to 300." And I made the count for the tanks. Of course I had to have some training. But the other guys, they wound up in the infantry. I figured I would have to have tank training, and I thought maybe, just maybe it'd be over by the time I got done, but no luck. I had to go to Blackdown. I transferred to Blackdown and that's where I got my tank training.*

INTERVIEWER: What position in the tank did you take on?

PAPA: *I'm a qualified gunner-operator. But there were two of us in the tank and we were both qualified gunner-ops and the sergeant, he said, "Which one of you wants to be the gunner?" Well of course we both wanted to be the gunner, so we flipped a coin. I lost. I was the loader and the wireless operator, which turned out was the best job anyway because the guy that was the gunner, he would have never made a good loader – he was too clumsy.*

INTERVIEWER: Could he shoot straight?

PAPA: *No, he couldn't hit a cow in the head with a snow shovel full of rice. I'm surprised we ever got back alive. He was not a good gunner. He was a good guy, but not a good gunner. He never had a firearm in his hands before he joined the army. He had no idea about it.*

INTERVIEWER: Where and when did you join the Sherbrooks?

PAPA: *I joined them just right after the Falaise Gap. We put the tank on a truck and we were just sailing right along. The Germans went into full retreat. Then we got to Belgium at the Leopold Canal. That's where I saw my first action. Oh, boy I remember that one. We went in with a full troop and our tank was the only one that came back. I'd never been so scared in my life. Fortunately we got out of that one. After that, it was just one every day after that. Action after action.*

INTERVIEWER: What rank were you at this point?

PAPA: *I never got any rank at all, I was always a private. Of course when I got to the tanks I was a trooper. I was offered a couple of stripes one time over in Europe, but they wanted me to be a crew commander and well, as the crew commander you have to stick your head out of the tank, so I said, "No, I've got a good job and I want to keep it."*

Grama, however, loved her memories of that time in her life, which may have been why she tucked the letters away.

"Are you kidding? What did they say?" I asked my mom in excitement.

"I don't know. I was too tired to read them, and it felt like I would be prying into their personal life," she replied.

"Well, I can't wait to see them when I come home in a few weeks," I said.

A few minutes after I got through the door, my mom showed me the letters. We spent the afternoon reading through them over a pot of tea. We laughed at her wit, we were touched by how much she longed to be with Papa, and we felt inspired by the ever-present sense of adventure that we knew and loved about her.

Reading them, I began to see my grandmother in a new way. In that moment, the letters were connecting us as women. I thought about the loss my mom had been through for the first time. I was 14 when my grandmother died in 1998, soon after having a stroke. I was most likely wrapped up in my own teenage dramas. I didn't really understand at the time what Mom went through.

"You can really feel her spirit in her words, can't you, Car?" my mom said with a smile, fondly remembering her mother's younger years.

It made us remember her strong British accent that she never lost, always being so cheerful and bubbly, and always wearing bright red lipstick, bold colours, and costume jewellery. It truthfully was the first time that I was putting two-and-two together of what being a war bride actually meant. I started thinking about what it was that she did for love. She moved across the ocean. It started to sink in what an incredible woman she was to give up her life in London, England, leave her family and friends and everything she knew, for the small town of Leamington, Ontario, Canada and follow love across the world.

At that time, I just so happened to be dating a British boy and he was helping me find documents in England that would help me get an ancestry visa someday. He helped me find a copy of my grandmother's birth certificate, marriage certificate, and other documents from my family history. My 24-year-old mind took it as a sign to do the same and decided to give my British boyfriend a chance. The letters were lovingly put aside as a treasured family memento.

Grama during World War II

CHAPTER 3

SEEKING

F inding my grandmother's letters motivated my mom and I, but in very different ways. My mom began connecting with family members she'd lost touch with, while the letters got me thinking about the love and sacrifice it took to maintain a long-term relationship. After giving it a chance, I ended up breaking up with my British boyfriend after all. I knew I needed to be on my own for a while and find out who I was and what I wanted. At 25, I was at the end of a third serious relationship. It was time for me to stand on my own two feet. I was single and bruised and a little ashamed that, instead of love letters, my leaving method of choice was usually a breakup letter.

At this time in my life, part of me felt like I was living in the movie 27 *Dresses*. All of my girlfriends were getting married. The wedding parties and parties that happen with weddings – engagement parties, bridal showers, bachelorettes, rehearsal dinners, the Big Day, and all of the planning and dress fittings in between – were my second full-time job. It was the stage of life we were at. Or I suppose I should say *they* were at. It was the stage of life everyone else was at, but me. I may or may not have been the single, bitter bridesmaid or maid of honour at a few too many of my friends' weddings, and I will admit that I regret a few speeches that were made.

I woke up one morning wanting more. I didn't exactly know where that more would come from, but I knew I needed to start asking questions. I was in a job that was okay, but not my passion. I wanted to be in a career of helping people that were going through a hard time, but knew I didn't want to go back to school. I had a cute apartment by the Detroit River and was single for the first time in 10 years and knew that I would someday want to share my life with someone, but knew that I needed to figure out who I was on my own first.

Travel and photography always made me feel alive. At this point, I had spent some time travelling Europe, the East and West coasts of Canada, tons of cities in the U.S. and two years teaching abroad in South Korea and travelling Asia. I loved the adventure, and I loved to photograph the colours of the world.

Because of the letters, my mom had gotten in touch with her cousin Michael who she hadn't seen in over 40 years and, after a year of corresponding, planned a reunion trip to New York for the fall for his daughter's Bat Mitzvah. When my parents asked me to tag along, I didn't hesitate. The girl who had been drawing the New York City skyline since she was old enough to hold a pen would never turn down a trip to NYC. We decided to head to Boston first and then take the train to NYC from there.

While in Boston visiting my parents' best friends Dan and Lauren, who were like an aunt and uncle to me, a conversation happened with Dan that made me realize there was more to me than working at my customer service day job. Dan was an innovative designer and travelled around the world teaching leadership and design thinking. I admired Dan and I wanted to be like him. We had long conversations about what I wanted to do.

There was depth, passion, curiosity, and a connection to life stories that was more than just a case of having an old soul. I knew that I needed to explore it more, and that I trusted and respected Dan so much that, when he suggested taking some coaching courses, I barely even read the course description and enrolled. All I needed to know was that it was about personal development, exploring values, and living a fulfilled life. The training was held in Toronto, Chicago, and California, giving me a great excuse to travel. That was enough for me.

The coaching courses led me to yet another enrollment into the world of leadership development, which was offered in California and consisted of four one-week retreats over a 10-month period. I went on a whim, borrowed some money from my parents, and booked my first of four flights from Detroit to San Francisco.

Over those 10 months, I discovered things about the way I showed up in this world that I worked on. My fidgetiness in the spotlight that would make my face turn beet-red, my crazed reaction to everything with the typical Canadian apology, and my obsession with feeling unworthy of being a leader at such a young age, seeing as I was the youngest in the course, some participants even four decades my senior.

At first, signs showed up subtly. The kind of nudge that makes you question if the life you are working toward was the one you wanted in the first place. It then transformed into opportunities arising that I couldn't help but say YES to. Enrolling in these courses and exploring my values, passion, and calling led me back to myself and the life stories of those that came before me.

CHAPTER 4

QUEEN MARY

The leadership program brought some pretty incredible people into my life. Mary was one of them, and the adventures we found ourselves on made me feel like a kid again – sing-alongs, fairies, magic and all. Mary was like no one I had ever known. She wore sweater capes, had a distinct American accent, and regularly talked of magic. She had childlike eyes and a giggle that made me smile. She seemed to notice the beautiful things around her and saw those things as a gift from God...even if it was a piece of a broken toy that had dropped to the ground. Mary calls herself Mary the Fairy who lives in a magical garden of joy. I felt like she was from another world, but something about her intrigued me the minute I met her. We connected through our shared passion for music and singing and looking for the simple joys around us.

During the second retreat, I popped into the bathroom during a break and was humming "Silver Bells" while I washed my hands. I heard someone in the stall behind me humming along. At the end of the song, she said, "Who's that?" in her high-pitched, childlike, let's-go-play-outside voice. Before we made it out of the bathroom, we had decided we were going to work together. We partnered up for the project that we were required to work on in between retreats. I returned home excited about what the next few months would bring and thrilled to have met a real-life fairy.

It wasn't long until I was boarding another plane to California. After our project for the course requirement was complete, we planned to hit the coastal highway and road trip our way up from San Diego to Sonoma just in time for our third retreat.

The road trip brought many unexpected surprises, including

the utter panic I felt when I realized that my phone map function wasn't working without WiFi and the only navigation system we had was a paper map from Texaco. The amount of times my finger and thumb instinctively tried to zoom in on that gas station map proved that we were in serious trouble if I was the co-pilot on this grand adventure.

"We're screwed," I exclaimed as I tossed the map into the back seat.

"Tink knows the way!" Mary said as she turned up Jackson 5 and started belting out "I'll Be There" with Michael himself.

Tink was her Lincoln, and Tink the Linc had just as much magic in her engine as Mary the Fairy did in her heart. The next thing I heard was Mary singing, "Tink, take us to a hotel." And before I could even fold up the crinkled map from the back seat, we turned the corner and pulled into a hotel parking lot. As Mary approached the front desk to check in and get us a room, I flipped through the pages of a local magazine where I came across a picture of the RMS Queen Mary.

"Excuse me, where is this ship?" I asked the hotel clerk.

"Oh, it's about 10 miles from here. It has been docked here since her last voyage in 1967," he said with a smile before promptly getting back to checking us in.

"This is the ship. This is the ship that my grandmother came to Canada on as a war bride," I said to no one in particular, not even sure if it was quite loud enough for anyone within earshot. Perhaps I was saying it to myself and out loud in disbelief.

I sat and scrolled through my photos on my phone and there it was, 20 photos back. On my most recent visit with my grandfather, I had just so happened to snap a picture of a photograph I had seen my entire life, a photograph that I had misunderstood or at least didn't completely understand. It was a picture of my grandmother and grandfather standing in front of the Queen Mary in Long Beach, California sometime in the 90s.

I knew my grandparents loved to travel. I knew my grandmother was British, but I hadn't quite thought about that specific voyage that she took on the Queen Mary in 1946.

"Mary, we gotta go to that ship tomorrow," I said as we walked down the hall to our hotel room.

"Tink will take us!" she exclaimed with a twinkle in her eye, as if she had already known something like this would happen.

As I wiggled my way into the tightly tucked bed sheets, I had one last look at the photo on my phone. I whispered to Mary how excited I was, but she was fast asleep. Morning couldn't have come fast enough.

The next morning, after I scarfed the continental breakfast down, I packed up my things in record time and was waiting at the car, jumping around like a lunatic.

We followed the road signs that read "Queen Mary tourist attraction".

"Do you want to go in?" Mary asked.

"No, I just need to find a spot by the fence at the front of the ship," I said as I speed-walked around the crowds.

I found the fence they stood in front of and lined myself up. I handed Mary the camera and gave her a quick rundown of how to hold it, position the shot, and focus the little square box on my head. I heard the SLR beep and snap and ran back over to her.

As I held the phone in one hand, the camera screen in the other, comparing the two side by side, something came alive in me. As I recreated that photo of my grandparents' years and a lifetime later, inspiration struck out of nowhere, and I knew I would be going to England.

Grama and Papa at Queen Mary

Carly at Queen Mary

CHAPTER 5

HOME TO PLAN

" Mom, I need those letters" were the first words to come out of my mouth when I barged into my childhood home.

"Well, hello to you too, Carly," my mom giggled, used to the lightning bolts of inspiration that were often hitting my father in the same sort of ways. "What for?"

"I have an idea," I stated.

I reached for the first letter of the pile and turned it over.

"Mom, can I use your iPad?"

She passed it over to me.

I opened up Google and transcribed the return address my grandmother had penned on the back of the airmail envelope into the search box. I clicked on maps and there it was, the bright red dot and the street view.

"Mom, the house is still there. The house Grama wrote the letters from still stands after all these years. Mom! I'm going to England!"

It was as if I could feel my grandmother's spirit urging me to go. She would have loved everything about this idea. My mom was sitting next to me engrossed in one of the letters.

"Of course you are Carly," she said once it finally sank in.

After my spur of the moment decisions to go to Korea...twice, travel through Europe, and the gallivanting I'd been doing since starting my coach training, nothing I did seemed to surprise her anymore. But this time, I could see that she was happy.

We spent the afternoon looking through the scrapbook my grandmother kept before she crossed the ocean to be with my grandfather. It was thick with ration books, wedding cards, her wedding invitation, telegrams she and Papa had exchanged, her immigration papers, and the welcome documents she'd received when she finally made it to her new home.

"When are these dated again?" I asked.

As I sorted through the letters and put them in order by date, I noticed they were from January to July of 1946. There were 110 of them, and they were written from my grandmother to my grandfather just after he and the other Canadian troops sailed back to Canada after the war. My grandmother was a British war bride and they were married in October of 1945, so these letters were from when they were married but apart as my grandmother waited for passage from the Canadian government along with 40,000 other wives.

I could retrace her steps and recreate her time in England. I could go to England and live for six months, separated from friends and family and my life as I knew it. I could follow her letters as much as I could. Do the things she did. Go to the shops and theatres. Eat at the restaurants she ate in. Wander the streets she called home. I was going to try to see London through my grandmother's eyes.

If the house was still there, maybe some of the other places she wrote about would be too. I could hear my grandmother's voice calling to me in the British accent she never lost, "*Pack your bags, Lovie. London is calling.*"

I started making plans. I started thinking about taking a leave of absence from the bank. I figured I would be ready for something big after my final leadership retreat that was coming up in June. I thought about how I would finance the trip, where I would live, and what I would do. I had come up with the idea to go for at least the duration of the letters, so January to July of 2013, which gave me exactly nine months to plan. I even realized that the 1946 and 2013 calendars matched up, so her Monday was going to fall on my Monday. It felt meant to be for so many reasons. I started talking about my idea to anyone who would listen. I had never been so sure of anything in my life. And nothing could stop me from going. Not even Prince Charming himself.

CHAPTER 6

PRINCE CHARMING

T he leadership program seemed to have given me the courage that I needed to start saying yes to things even if they
scared me. Singing in public again was one of them, and this is
how I found myself rehearsing with my friend Matt as we prepared to perform at The Last Friday Coffee House. My dad was a
well-known local musician and hosted a monthly gathering place
for musicians to play three songs each at a local restaurant's basement café. Music was in my blood after all, and I figured that, with
Matt's crazy talent and my experience from my high school vocal
jazz, choir, and pageant days, we'd be golden.

I had told a lot of people to come and announced it on Facebook. Some friends and colleagues came from the city, and lots of
my dad's regulars were there to cheer us on. Also in the crowd that
night was one of Matt's roofing buddies, Adam. I knew him as the
nice guy from high school that played lots of sports, but I hadn't
really interacted with him much, if ever.

Being the daughter of the host and from a small town, I was
a natural chatterbox and smiled and said hello to a lot of people,
even if their names slipped my mind. I worked off my nerves by
working the crowd, and as I circled the tables doing my rounds
before the show, I thanked Adam for coming and, in my nervous
small talk, brushed his arm and told him that it was nice to see
him. The courage was apparently then passed on to him, because
later that night this message came through on Facebook:

March 30, 2012
Adam

"Hey Carly.
I don't think I told you tonight but great job. You were fantastic!!! Shoot me a line when you want to talk about London and I will impart whatever wisdom I have. Hahaha"

I remember it making me smile at the time, but I was so into my own stuff that I forgot to reply.

A month later, we ran into each other again at Katie and Matt's house, and the next night, another message came through.

May 7, 2012
Adam

"Hey you, So I hear you might be joining our book club for this scandalous 50 Shades of Gray book we are reading. That is great!!! Thanks for the beers on Saturday too. It was great seeing you. Talk to you later."

I replied immediately after noticing that I still hadn't replied to his first message a month before. *Oops.*

I promptly messaged him back and from there our regular chats began and the crushes started developing. Katie and Matt had another get-together the next weekend and I was pretty excited for the potential to see him again. We played beach volleyball and had a great time. I was covered in sand and jumped into the shower,

and by the time I got out, he was leaving. It was then that I realized that I liked him. I hadn't talked about England much, because I didn't know how excited he'd be about getting involved with someone who would be leaving so soon and be gone for so long.

With every text message exchange I liked him more. I couldn't believe this was happening. Right when I was starting to actually enjoy being single and on my own for the first time in 10 years and now, right as I was planning my trip to England, this fabulous guy drops into my life.

It made me think of how Grama and Papa met. From the stories that I heard growing up from both of them, this is how I imagined it.

Fresh from the bath, Rene was ready for a diversion. She had spent the last week taking apart a German spy plane. When she had seen the ad in the library six months ago, recruiting women to work at the Farnborough Royal Aircraft Establishment an hour southwest of London, she had been intrigued and excited. It was the middle of World War II, and the opportunity for women to serve was a rare bright spot among the challenges that came from living in wartime London. Another benefit had been escaping the nightly bombing raids that plagued London, but she felt guilty knowing that her mom and sister would continue to spend many of their nights sleeping in the underground.

In all the time she had been here, she'd never seen the girls she worked with in such a tizzy. A group of Canadian soldiers had been temporarily assigned to the small town of Farnborough before they shipped out to France the next day. Conveniently, these soldiers found themselves in close proximity to a clatter of single British ladies who made their way to the cinemas, canteens, and dance halls after work. The gramophones and live bands had been working overtime since the Canadian troops arrived, setting the tone for the hopeful wartime love and romance that permeated the air. Rene was older than most of the girls there. At 24, she was pushing the limits of prime marriage material, and the war had reduced the pool of eligible men to a trickle. Rene had given up on love, but she wasn't a pessimist. She'd go out with the girls and have fun because you never know.

When they entered the dance hall, they had to push their way past a group of soldiers celebrating a birthday. She glanced at the birthday soldier. Tall, handsome, and a bit tipsy from the free beers and backslaps. Rene summoned up her courage and asked him for a dance. He smiled, pulled himself up a bit taller, and introduced himself, putting out a hand.

"Hi. I'm Nick, but I'm not much of a dancer," he said with a smile.

He kept his eye on the bold brunette for the rest of the night, and when the time was right, he offered to walk her home. He was shipping out the next day and he couldn't think of a better way to spend his last night of leave than chatting up a British beauty. As they walked through the backstreets lit by the occasional glow of a streetlamp, their jokes and laughter echoed along the cobblestoned streets.

When they arrived at her billet, the soldier closed his eyes for a kiss, swaying a bit from the birthday beers. After a few

Right, women mechanics carting more flying bomb salvage to the dump.

Rene in the newspaper

34

seconds of silence, he opened his eyes, and as things came back into fo-
cus he realized that she had run up the stairs and was gone. He heard a
"Cheerio, darling" reverberating down the staircase. With a little sigh and
a shrug of his shoulders, he smiled and headed back to camp.

A week or so later, he noticed a name and address tucked in the pock-
et of his uniform. His buddies assured him it belonged to the mysterious
staircase runaway from the night of his birthday, Rene. He hadn't stopped
thinking about her since that night. Her laugh rang through his memory
and brought a smile to his face on the hardest of days. He wrote her a let-
ter. That was the beginning of a love story that lasted 65 years.

My first date with Adam wasn't the greatest. It was awkward and I was to blame. I talked way too fast and way too much. At this point in time, I had been on several blind dates and setups through friends. You would think that I was getting closer to mastering the first date jitters with every date I would go on, but no...not this girl. I bombed it. It was awful, just like the rest. It did feel different though. He somehow stayed interested. It was like he could see through the awkward, or even kind of liked it.

I knew for sure that he wasn't into game playing, so that was reassuring. In some of our first exchanges over email, he gave me his number and the area code seemed weird. When I asked him about it, this was his response: "No, I do not live in Detroit or Timbuktu – maybe dream of living there sometimes – so you are right, the area code is 226, not 336 and I promise I wasn't trying to drop you a fake number. That is not my game – if I have any game." I knew at the end of it all he would be straight with me. He would tell me thanks but no thanks probably right to my face.

He picked me up in a big manly truck. That in itself makes any small town girl swoon. We went to Nikko Sushi in Kingsville. I had borrowed a dress from Jenny who lives in the apartment below me but realized five minutes before I left that it was too tight. I threw on some jeans and a tank top and hoped for the best.

What made us stay afloat was our connection to great people. My childhood friend Melissa married his brother Brad, and Katie and Matt were two of our favourite people. There had to be something special here. We decided to see past the awkward. It got a little worse, then quickly better when we decided to unexpectedly show up at Katie and Matt's that night. Showing up together of course made for a pretty confused greeting as we strolled up to their porch.

"Oh hey guuuuys!?" they stated and questioned at the same time, slowly putting two-and-two together. Laughing through the awkward together, the four of us made it all seem bearable.

He dropped me off at home that night, no kiss, but the world's best hug. I'm sure he could probably feel my shoulders lower the second we were reminded that something had brought us together that was worth believing in.

Our second date was better and was shared over Wendy's Frosties. My tone had come down a notch, I was speaking at a normal pace, and I actually thought about the words before they came out of my mouth. We talked about everything, maybe even for the second time, but this time I slowed down enough to notice his smile, his beautiful brown eyes, and his gorgeous manly beard.

Shortly after our second date, I came home from work to find Adam sitting on the stoop of my building waiting for me. I had planned to spend the evening with my friend Meaghan planning our trip to San Francisco. I was heading to California for my last leadership retreat, and Meaghan was going to join me on the front end of the trip. But, when I turned the corner and saw Adam sitting there, I immediately called Meaghan as I parked the car telling her, "I need to reschedule. There is a boy on my stoop!"

We spent the evening talking and eating frozen pizza. Much like my grandmother, I wasn't the best cook. I figured I might as well be upfront about it rather than have him find out down the road and be disappointed I wasn't a fan of cooking shows or being adventurous in the kitchen. If it was just me, I could eat the same few things every few days and couldn't even fathom cooking a three-course meal. Luckily, his dad was the cook of the family, and he had passed it down to his kids, so turns out my weekly meals were about to expand to much more impressive things like scallops and steak and fancy breakfasts and all.

That was the night we started falling in love. We spent a lot of time together. We met each other's families. Things moved fast.

I had another wedding in July. This time, I wasn't going stag. I invited Adam to go with me. The wedding was in Connecticut. We drove down from Windsor. There was no denying that this was a test.

At the border between Canada and the U.S., we were pulled over and taken inside for questioning. We were put in separate rooms and quizzed. As we were pulling the car around, he said, "Oh by the way, my name is Micheal." Even though that came as a shock to me, having known him all throughout high school as the jock named Adam with frosted tips, his legal name was the least of our worries. Turns out, I hadn't told him enough details of the courses I had been taking in California.

Border Patrol questions: Whose wedding are you going to? How do you know these people? What kind of a course did you take? Did you have a student visa? How did you pay for it? What do you do for a living?

My answers: "My friend's name is Lisa. She's marrying Seth. I met her through a leadership course. It's through the Coach Training Institute. It's a life coaching, personal development, and leadership organization based out of San Rafael, California. They train people to identify ways to live a life of purpose, connection, fulfillment, self-expression, and leadership. I didn't need a student visa to take the course. I took a loan from my parents. I work at a bank. Seriously...do you have Google on that computer, officer? Search for The Coach Training Institute. CTI. It's all there."

Adam's answers: "Uhhh. We just started dating. I don't really know what the course is all about. It sounds really great though."

Lisa, one of my friends from leadership training, was the bride, and she had asked me to sing in her wedding. The whole way there I practiced the song, in between pauses in our deep conversation. Adam listened to the song over and over again. At the reception, while I was singing, I spotted him in the doorway holding our drinks, smiling at me cutely, and singing along. Most men would have been sick of the song by then, but not Adam.

Up until the road trip, we hadn't really talked. Not in the way I wanted to. I wanted deep conversation. I wanted to talk about values, our deal breakers, what was important to each of us, what kind of life we wanted to live. I could usually talk about all of this stuff very easily, but with Adam it was harder. I had to initiate the conversations. He didn't need to know. It was as if he knew we were meant for each other. I was the one that was slower figuring that out.

At the end of the wedding on a beautiful hilltop, we all released lanterns. Before this moment whenever I had a chance to make a wish – on birthday candles, on significant times like 11:11 – I wished for happiness. All through my previous relationships that was what I wanted. Just to be happy. But that night, I wished for more of this. For more of what Adam and I were creating and experiencing. I wondered, standing there, watching my lantern drift skyward, was this happy?

A few weeks later, lying in bed so sick I could barely raise my head, I found out what Adam had wished for that night. My throat hurt, my sinuses were a mess, and I was disgusting. Adam came over and told me to rest and that he would be right back. When he came back, he had cold medicine, orange juice, chicken noodle soup, and yellow flowers. He brought the flowers over and I told him I couldn't believe how nice he was and how disgusting I was. That was when I told him I loved him. He then went on to tell me that he knew he already loved me, but he wanted to hear it from me first. That had been his lantern wish.

Once we started dating, I stopped talking about my plans to move to London for a little while, but in my mind I was always going and continued to take steps toward making it happen behind the scenes. I applied for a leave from work, I gave notice on my apartment, and started thinking about what I would sell and what I would store in my parents' basement. We talked about the trip a little bit here and there, but we were so wrapped up in falling in

Adam and Carly
dating

love that we were able to put it in the back of our minds for the time being.

I should have known that when you make this kind of commitment and decision to yourself, that naturally things start happening around you that reiterate that this is exactly what you were meant to do even when those things include both the incredibly perfect and inconvenient timing to fall in love. It seemed that within seconds of committing to the trip and the journey, there were bigger plans in the works. It was hard to believe that our paths just so happened to cross after being worlds apart in years prior. It was the classic "right place, right time" sort of love, that in hindsight, a matter of days or even hours could have changed the fate of us coming together.

The more sure I felt about our relationship, the bigger London loomed. A few months before I was set to leave, we started to realize it was real. The planning and logistics started in full force, and I knew deep down that he had been super supportive and loving since day one. I finally worked up the courage to have a conversation about London. I knew we had to start really talking about how this would work for us.

"I'm leaving for London soon. I have to go," I said

Adam said, "I know. Maybe I'll find a way to come too."

That was a possibility I hadn't thought about. Whether he came or not though, I knew that I had to go.

CHAPTER 7

MY LIFE'S LETTER

In August, I applied for an ancestry visa. I didn't technically need one for the kind of trip I was taking, but it was the novelty of the ancestry visa I was going for. It would enable me to work in the UK if I chose to do so and would permit me to stay for five years if I wanted. I loved applying for the ancestry visa, digging up all of the documents to prove my ancestry and tracking down the birth certificates for myself, my mom, and my grandmother. Finding her marriage certificate and passport made the adventure I was starting real. It made me feel connected to her. The more I found out about her, the more I wanted to know.

By September I finally asked for yet another leave of absence from the bank. When I asked, my boss rolled her eyes, but I didn't blame her. This was the third time I had requested a leave throughout my career. By now, I was sure that she was expecting it.

I wanted to write about my experiences in London so I started brainstorming names for the blog. For me, my grandmother's letters had become more than just letters from a new wife to her husband an ocean away. They were life lessons. They were a window into the kind of love story that I wanted. On October 30, 2012, my grandparents' wedding anniversary, I wrote my first blog for "Life's Letter."

I made business cards with the website and a pretty image of Grama's cursive to hand out to people I met along the way so they would know where to find me. At the end of November, it was time to move out of my apartment that I loved so much. I was going to stay with my brother Ryan and his wife Sulienne through the holidays and then leave for London right after the New Year.

Leaving my apartment was harder than I could have imagined. Seeing my distress, the nice guy who was scheduled to move in the next day asked if I wanted one more night in the apartment. I did. I needed to say goodbye. The apartment was perfect. It had high ceilings, hardwood floors, crown molding, a cozy fireplace, a second-floor patio, and a great view. It was of Detroit, which was right across the river from Windsor, but if I tilted my head and squinted, it looked just like the New York City skyline. I spent the evening walking through the apartment one room at a time, thanking the space and saying goodbye. And then I crawled onto the futon, the only piece of furniture left in the apartment, and cried. I did a lot of growing up in that apartment. I discovered so much about who I was, who I wanted to be, and who I was not. They were my two years of self-discovery and personal growth. I learned that I always want to be learning, taking risks, and trying new things. Creating every day, loving with my whole heart, and having the courage to live my dreams.

As I pulled away from the apartment the next day, I looked in the rearview mirror. I was more sad than when I moved away for university. This was the place I grew into myself. It was the place I had found the best parts of me. The me I wanted to be, not the me I had been. It was where Adam and I had gotten to know one another and where we told each other "I love you" for the first time. I knew driving away a part of my life was ending and as excited as I was for what was ahead, I would miss that girl who worked so hard to figure out who she was.

CHAPTER 8

BON VOYAGE

N ews travels fast in small towns. People started asking me about my trip. When was I leaving? How long would I be gone? Why London? I started handing out the business cards with my blog on it and telling people to be sure to follow my project and my trip while I was away. I was so excited and I wanted to stay in touch with my family, friends, co-workers, and customers.

My dad had a friend who worked at our hometown paper *The Southpoint Sun,* who, after looking at my blog, thought it would make a good story. After the article came out, I made copies and started handing them out with my card to customers and anyone who would listen. One of those people just so happened to be a writer for *The Windsor Star.* He expressed interest and later picked up my story and asked to do a photo shoot.

A few days later, I showed up to my appointment with the re-porter at the newspaper headquarters in downtown Windsor. I checked in at the front desk and walked through the open concept office cubicles and noticed the gorgeous floor-to-ceiling windows overlooking the city center. I passed what I imagined to be the conference room where they decide on what headlines will run for the next day's news. The reporter took notes in his small notebook, had a recorder on for our conversation, and told me that he was hoping to write a long article about my upcoming trip.

The photo shoot was next. The photographer grabbed his cam-era bag and told me to follow him. I was happy that he decided to take some shots outside so that I could wear my red coat. The colour red always reminded me of my grandmother. It was her fa-vourite colour. We started walking small side streets and eventually turned down an alley. He pointed to the raggedy brick wall and said, "Voila! The perfect backdrop for this shoot." He had me hold up my grandmother's scrapbook with the letters on display being held up with the hand that was wearing my grandmother's ring. It only took about 10 minutes, a few different poses here, a move of the letter position there, and we were done.

Windsor woman sets off on epic journey in her grandmother's footsteps

Windsor Star – Trevor Wilhelm – January 3, 2013

Wearing her grandmother's ring on her right hand, Carly Butler holds a book of telegrams and a stack of letters written by her grandmother and grandfather during WWII December 19, 2012.

The seeds for Carly Butler's life-changing adventure were sown 40 years before she was born.

Butler is setting out next week to retrace the footsteps of her grandmother, a war bride who counted the days until she could leave her worn-torn English home to join her new husband in Leamington.

After her grandmother Irene Wiebe died, and her grandfather Nick moved to a retirement home, their family discovered letters the young war bride sent during six agonizing months they spent with an ocean between them.

"It brought her back to life for us," said Butler, 27. "We could feel her spirit. We could giggle about some of the things she said. She always had that British accent that everybody was so curious about. She was very bubbly and bold. Reading them brought that back."

The love that lasted a lifetime began with a three-day courtship. Nick Wiebe was born in Russia, but his Mennonite family moved to Leamington when he was two years old. In 1939, after Nazi Germany invaded Poland, Canada declared war.

Nick signed up, even though Mennonites had special exemptions from having to fight. "He wanted to prove that he was a good Canadian, because he lived in Canada his whole life," said Butler.

Nick was a tank loader and wireless operator in the Sherbrooke Fusilier Regiment, which fought throughout northwestern Europe. In the summer of 1945, he was granted a leave and went to London. Irene Fineberg lived there, working at a factory dismantling airplanes.

"It's hard to imagine my grandma taking apart planes," said Butler. "I have a picture of her from an article in a paper, carrying a big plane with a bunch of other women."

They ended up at the same dance hall. There were sparks. They danced all night. Then he walked her home.

"He went to give her a hug, and she was gone," said Butler.

Two weeks later, Nick was doing his laundry. He found Irene's name and address in a coat pocket. She had slipped it in there without him knowing.

He started writing to her. On his next leave, he went to see her.

"After three days, he asked her to marry him," said Butler.

The love-struck couple was married Oct. 30, 1945. But the war was over. Nick eventually had to ship back home. Irene stayed behind. "She was waiting for her papers, because she was a British war bride," said Butler. "So they were married but apart for six months."

Longing to stay connected to her new husband, the young war bride picked up a pen. The collection of about 100 letters began in January 1946.

She wrote about food rationing, going to the movies, riding the subway and other little moments from her days.

"A customer made me laugh this morning, she came in the shop and said 'Rene I read in the paper yesterday that 900 brides left for Canada, why haven't you gone?'" she wrote on April 9th, 1946. "She nearly fainted when I told her there was 40,000 of us all together."

Irene also wrote about how she missed her new husband and how she couldn't wait to join him in Canada.

"Today I saw Leamington on a map and I got really excited," she wrote.

On July 19, 1946, after a long ocean ride aboard the Queen Mary, Irene landed in Halifax. The pair remained together and in love until she died 14 years ago.

Nick went into a care home in 2009. While going through his belongings, Butler's mother Judy found the letters he'd kept and cherished for six decades.

There were also scrapbooks, telegrams, cards, boarding passes, and even the log book Butler's grandfather kept as a tank operator. One of his last entries is scribbled on the inside cover.

"Enemy retiring armistice signed war is over."

Butler immediately knew she wanted to do something with the letters, to honour her grandparents. She just wasn't sure what she might do.

Then last February, she was in California. The Queen Mary happened to be docked there. Butler has a photo of her grandparents standing in front of the ship years after Irene arrived.

"I found the exact same spot that they stood, the fence where it lined up," said Butler. "I stood there and took a picture."

That was the genesis of her plan to spend six months in Europe. She took a leave of absence from work, took out a loan and is trying to raise money through an online video.

"Something came alive in me when I was there," said Butler. "I was like, 'This is cool.' My grandma stood in the exact same spot. She was looking at this ship thinking 'I took that over so many years ago.' It was cool to just see the ship and feel I was actually in a spot that my grandma had stood before. I need to go to England."

She will visit the home her grandmother lived in, the cinema she went to, the subway line she travelled, the city hall where her grandparents were married. While she's gone, she will post blogs at www.lifesletter.com. She hopes to turn her adventures into a book after she returns.

"The reason I get so excited about it is this is something only I can tell," said Butler. "It's unique. Not a lot of people have this, the gift of these letters. It's almost like I have to. It's part of keeping this history alive."

The interest in my project continued to snowball. Around the time the article came out, CTV Canada's largest television network called and wanted to do a story. I couldn't believe the attention

Grama's letters and my trip were getting. The story was bigger than I had ever imagined it would be. My blog was getting views from around the world. By mid-December, I had 1,000 visits and I hadn't even left yet.

When my CTV interview rolled around, I was pacing around the living room of the house I grew up in, looking down the street every few minutes to see if the reporter was close. I was nervous, but glad it wasn't live. When I was getting ready, Adam went downstairs to print the notes I had made. When he came back, he handed me a stack of paper. On top was a sheet of paper with flight information on it. Why had he printed off my flight information? It took me a minute to figure out it was for *his* flight. To my disbelief and soon after delight, I realized he had surprised me with the gift of joining me on this journey. His plan was to come with me to London for the first week to help me find a place and get myself set up and familiar with the neighbourhood I would be spending a lot of time in. It was a fantastic surprise. I was overjoyed. He was going to come with me. Adam was full of surprises. And this would not be his last.

Gina was the CTV reporter, and she put me at ease the second she got out of her car. She had been texting me all morning about the weather. The drive to Leamington from Windsor could be treacherous after a snowfall. When we met her at the door, it felt like a long-lost friend had come to visit. Her enthusiasm about my story and my upcoming trip was contagious. It actually started to sink in for me all over again when I started to tell her my story. I even almost forgot about the big camera in the corner catching our every move. It felt so comfortable talking to her. She asked questions about how we found the letters, how I came up with the idea, my plans for England, and she even asked my mom a few questions on camera. We stopped by the senior home my grandfather was living in and asked him if he wanted to be on TV with us. He was more than happy to share his story, so Gina came and shot a few scenes of the three generations talking about my trip.

The radio interview at Mix 96.7 was next and was way more

relaxed. The music was pumping when I walked in, the hosts were calm, cool, and collected, like one would imagine, and my eye caught the ON AIR box that lights up like you see in the movies. I had met Justin, the radio host through a high school friend, and he invited me to come by two days before I left. His 6'5" stature, natural booming voice, and super goofy antics immediately put me at ease. This interview was live, so the pressure was on to not stumble over ummms and likes, but I did surprisingly okay. I had been behind a mic like this before, when my dad had us record backup vocals for a local commercial he was making, but this time, it was just me and the host. We talked about my journey, the letters, leaving my sweetheart behind, and the excitement of the adventure.

I also started an Indiegogo campaign. Indiegogo was one of the first crowdfunding sites. The way it worked was I put up my project and if people were interested, they could donate to support my trip. I had heard about crowdfunding from a friend of mine from California, and Indiegogo was Canadian friendly, so I decided to go for it. I called up a friend to shoot a video, came up with some perks for supporters, and calculated just how much this year would cost me. Any help I could get was gravy. One of the perks I offered was to send everyone who contributed postcards and letters.

Between all the media hoopla and the holidays, my last few weeks at home flew by. Adam and I spent our first Christmas together. We spent New Year's at Adam's parents' house. My parents came, and we had a Mexican-themed gathering. My dad came dressed to impress in his sombrero, guitar, and colourful poncho, and the rest of us brought themed food. We played games, ate great Mexican cuisine, and rang in the New Year by hitting wooden spoons on pot and pans while running down the street to Adam's grandparents' house.

As I sat and watched everyone around me, I couldn't help but see my future unfolding. In my heart, I knew this was the first of many holiday seasons together as a big family. I could just feel it.

My ancestry visa finally came on December 29th. It was a relief. I had a plan B, a working holiday visa that I could have applied

Papa as a soldier and Papa in 2013

for if the ancestry hadn't come through or I could have just gone as a tourist and hoped for the best, but having the ancestry visa made staying and possibly working in England for an extended period much easier. Standing there, holding the visa in my hands made it *real*. It was official. I was official, and I was going on this trip not just for fun but to discover my past.

I booked my flight for January 13 2013. If I let myself sit with my emotions for longer than five minutes, I was quick to realize that there were many of them. I was excited, nervous, anxious, and ready. I was sad that I was going to be apart from Adam for so long, but was mostly just looking forward to the adventure. I was so busy throughout these days and weeks, soaking up time with

Adam, family, and friends, organizing all of the fine details, such as loans and leaves, and cleaning out my locker at work that it was hard to really feel everything.

My last day of work was January 4th. I think most of my co-workers were pushing me out the door with love, with equal parts support and relief that the time had finally come. They had heard my story on repeat for the past six months and were incredibly skilled at putting up with scatterbrained antics in my final days there – the worst of them being my sneaking out the back-door to watch my CTV coverage at the deli around the corner on my last shift.

Right before I left for London, I met with Marty Gervais about working on a book. He was my co-worker's professor, and she knew that he would love my story. I was intimidated about meeting with Canada's Poet Laureate and the author of numerous books, and a sought-after speaker. Partially bald, with a salt-and pepper-beard, wearing round glasses over very kind eyes, Marty immediately put me at ease.

I had Grama's letters to show him and I explained my trip. He told me I should write a book. I told him I wasn't sure that I was a writer. I loved journaling and blogging and had been keeping blogs when I went on previous trips but a book!? I had no idea how to even get started.

Marty told me to keep it simple and told me to write about what I see, hear, and feel every day. He also advised me not to take a writing course as it would just confuse me and add noise when really I just needed to pay attention and experience everything to its fullest.

Marty's support didn't stop there; he helped me apply for a writing grant through the Ontario Arts Council and also invited me to join his students in France to speak to his class and participate in the writing retreat he was hosting that summer at the end of my time in England. He was also the genius behind the idea of writing letters to my grandmother on my blog about what I was experiencing.

Meeting Marty confirmed a big lesson I had been learning since starting my coach training. Asking is scary, but what you might get is priceless. If I had stopped myself from asking Marty for help simply because of who he was, I would have missed out on one of the most important experiences and relationships connected to my journey. I vowed to never shy away from making the big ask.

CHAPTER 9

LONDON CALLING

A t long last, the day had finally come to board the plane to my grand adventure. It was officially about to begin. The flight from Toronto to Manchester was like any other flight, but it held that special magic that accompanies the cusp of a journey that was about to unfold. I had been thinking about this moment for months. I had put all of my focus and energy into being here and the moment had finally come.

It was hard to believe. When I first conceived of this trip, I was alone. I was going to make it alone. But now, I was boarding the plane with Adam, a man I felt certain was the real deal.

After we boarded the plane, I looked at my grandmother's letters to remind me of what the trip was all about. For the rest of the flight, in between stolen kisses with my sweetheart, we talked about my vision for the trip and my hopes and dreams for the next six months. My plan was to spend my time just as my grandmother had. Every Monday, I would sit down with the letters for that week and plan my days to follow Grama's adventures around London. If she went to Piccadilly Circus on Wednesday, that's where I would go. If she went to Shepherd's Bush or Kilburn High Street, I would head there too. I flipped through the calendar I had arranged, smiling down at the yellow stars that marked the date of each letter. I gazed out the window and whispered a quick thank you to my grandmother from above the clouds.

We landed at the Manchester airport and caught a bus from Manchester to Birmingham. My lifelong friend Elyse and her British husband Alec met us with open arms and big smiles. Elyse and I went way back to first grade and had the strongest bond. Elyse met

Alec in Korea while we were all teaching there, and he quickly became a long-lost brother to me. The second he heard that I had an older brother, he swooped in and started teasing and bothering me, and ruffling my feathers like all good older brothers do. Elyse and Alec's love was rare and beautiful, its foundation built on laughter and joy. They were always out having a great time, playing games and loving life. Their wedding was part of the 15 in two years that I went to single, but I behaved a bit better at their wedding. I marveled at how easy they were with one another. Bantering back and forth, making us feel right at home, telling me I could stay for as long as I wanted, as long as I kept the fridge stocked with cider. That sounded like reasonable rent to me.

We went for some pints at the local pub in Mosely and came back to their house to play cards. The house was an elegant looking British home. It was a six-story, red-brick, semi-detached Victorian home, with a large yard by England standards, backing onto a private park. The park was gated and had a large gorgeous pond and play area for kids, a soccer field, and nature trails. I felt extremely blessed to not only have an incredible place to land the first little while there, but to also be welcomed by a best friend and her hubby. It brought me so much comfort in that moment.

They drove us into London the next day. I was anxious to get to the big city, the place I would call home for the next six months. The closer we got to London, the more I felt my uneasiness rising. There were so many unknowns ahead. I was nervous. As I took a deep breath and took my first step onto London soil, I noticed a 5-pence coin. For as long as I could remember, my mother always told me that Grama would say when you find money, it means someone is giving you a sign. Since my grandmother passed, that was something that my mom and I always shared. Any time either of us found money, we would both share a glance and know in our hearts that it was Grama giving us a sign. Finding the coin immediately put me at ease.

Adam and I had arranged to stay at a rental flat in Turnham Green for four nights while I got my bearings and looked for a more permanent place to stay. Turnham Green was a lovely neighbourhood and every day we were there, we were greeted with a light dusting of snow that created the most magical layer on all things London – the bright red phone booths, the double- decker buses, and the brick fences that lined the tiny yards in front of the brownstones. It was picturesque and I was thrilled to be sharing this magical beginning with Adam.

The day finally came to officially start retracing my grandmother's steps. Her first letter was dated January 17 1946.

CHAPTER 10

GRAMA'S FIRST LETTER

F rom the day I first read Grama's letters and googled the address, my plan had been to take the subway to her tube stop, wander through her neighbourhood, find the house she wrote the letters from, and knock on the door. And there I was finally, standing in front of the door, turning over the fragile airmail envelope, looking at the address neatly penned in her handwriting. I couldn't believe that I was actually standing there. Before knocking, I glanced at the address one last time to be sure that the stranger's door I was about to knock on was the right one. I finally got the courage to knock and from inside the house, I could hear footsteps nearing the door. When the door opened, my emotions got the better of me, and all I could say to the woman standing there was, "My grandmother used to live here," as I held out the letter as proof.

I managed to compose myself, telling her my name and what had brought me to London, to this cobblestoned neighbourhood and to her front door. I was here to find out more about my grandmother, Rene, who had passed away in 1998. I explained that we found her love letters she had written to my grandfather in 1946, tucked away in a cupboard. I believed she hoped we would find them someday. And for me they had been a gift, one that had inspired me to come here and learn as much as I could about her and the city she loved.

This would be the first but not the last time on this trip I would see how fate weaves its magic. The woman at the door carried my grandmother's name. Renee was from New York; she and her husband had just bought the place a few months earlier. He was here on business, working for Apple. She instantly fell in love with my story and let us in.

Renee was blonde, petite, and very sweet. She told us about her family, her two kids, and what life had been like since moving to England. She told me about a woman that she knew who had lived in the neighbourhood the longest and took down my contact information to put me in touch with her. She had just met me and wanted to help me dig up clues from the past. She thought maybe they would remember my grandmother or at least be able to describe the neighbourhood and what it was like to live here then. She showed us around the house, told us about the renovations they had done, and even brought us upstairs.

The second we left I was high on life. I was literally walking down the street clicking my heels like Dick Van Dyke in *Mary Poppins*. I couldn't believe how nice Renee had been. I knew this was just the beginning of many magical things to come, and the connection I felt to Grama was so strong. I could picture her so much clearer now. It was like I could feel her energy in her streets.

After seeing her house and meeting Renee, I wanted to share the excitement that came from exploring the first letter with everyone back home. I spent much of the next morning in our rental flat window seat writing my first "Dear Grama" letter and posting it on my blog.

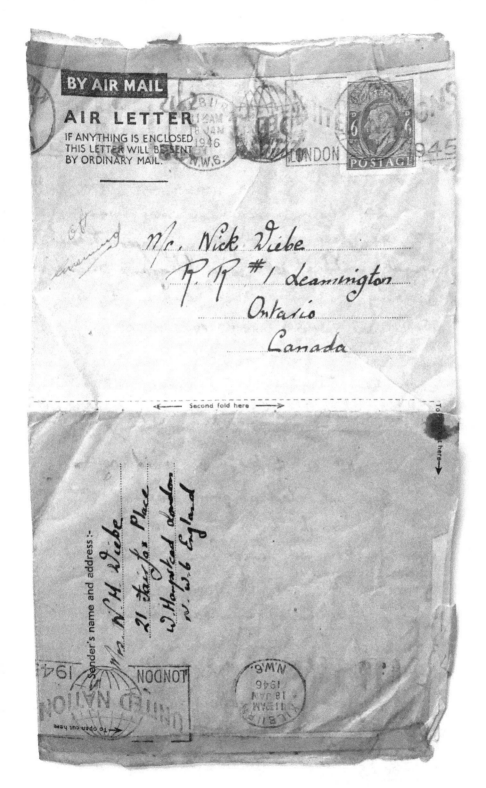

BY AIR MAIL

AIR LETTER

IF ANYTHING IS ENCLOSED
THIS LETTER WILL BE SENT
BY ORDINARY MAIL.

Mr. Nick Wiebe
R.R. #1 Leamington
Ontario
Canada

Second fold here

Sender's name and address :-

Mrs. N.H. Wiebe
21 Fairfax Place
W. Hampstead London
N.W.6 England

17/1/46

My Darling, I haven't written before because
I knew it wouldn't be any use as the
letter would get there before you. Darling, I
miss you terribly, more much more than I
ever did before, now I am only living
for the day when I get my papers & sail.
Right until I got your telegram Tuesday
morning, I thought and lived in the hope
that you would walk in once more
for a few stolen hours, but after I
got the telegram I knew you had gone.
Thanks for sending it darling, it was
sweet of you, if I hadn't of got it I
might still be thinking you would come.
I hope you had a good sailing darling
and it wasn't too rough (or does
that make you laugh) anyway the main
important thing is that you got there
safely. P.G. Everything back here is
very much the same, I started work
back again to-day at Samuel's, I couldn't
stay at home doing nothing any longer,
the time just seemed to drag. I wrote

58

and asked for[2] the address of the
Canadian Wives Club and I've got it
now, they met every first Monday in
the month and the next meeting is on
Feb 4th so I'm going to go and learn some
more about Canada and Canadian
cooking (Ha! Ha! that's not funny). It's a
funny thing darling but you know all
the time you was here we never heard
our song once, well both last night
and the night before I heard some one
singing it on the AFN, they must know
just how I feel. Every time I go in
our room, I nearly start crying and
it's worse when I go to bed, the
moon is still shining on our bed
just like it was the last night you
were here. On Tuesday night I went
to the Odeon and saw "love letters"
it was a lovely film and reminded
me so much of how letters brought us
to-gether. I'm going to Oxford on Sat
for the week-end to take Vera
back her things, any way it will make
a change for me, I'm going to take

59

my camera and take some snaps to send to you. That reminds me I bought a smashing photo album the other day and I've put in all my snaps but there is still a lot of room, so I'm ready for all the snaps you are going to send me. Now all I want is a scrap-book. One of the woman in the shop to-day asked me what I would like for a wedding present so I guess we are still collecting 'em. While I am writing this Dixie is walking all over the room, so you can just imagine. mmmm. I haven't answered Nanny's letter yet but I will soon, I have written to everybody else. Well darling I guess that about all for now, except that I love you and I won't feel like a whole person again until we are to-gether for good. P.S. Half of me is with you, well cheerio darling, God Bless you, and all the luck in the world to you. Au-revoir all my love forever

I LOVE YOU

your adoring wife

Rene

P.S. Give my love to the family.

January 17, 1946

My Darling,
I hadn't written before because I knew it wouldn't be any use as the letter would get there before you. Darling, I miss you terribly, much more than I ever did before now. I am only living for the day when I get my papers to sail. Right until I got your telegram Tuesday morning, I thought and lived in the hope that you would walk in once more for a few stolen hours, but after I got the telegram I knew you had gone...I hope you had a good sailing darling...the most important thing is that you got there safely...I wrote and asked for the address of the Canadian Wives Club and I've got it now, they meet every first Monday in the month and the next meeting is on February 4th so I am going to go and learn some more about Canada and Canadian cooking (haha, that's not funny)...On Tuesday night I went to the Odeon & saw "Love Letters" it was a lovely film and reminded me so much of how letters brought us together. I'm going to Oxford on Saturday for the weekend...it will make a change for me, I'm going to take my camera and take some snaps to send to you...Well darling I guess that's about all for now, except that I love you and I won't feel like a whole person again until we are together for good. Half of me is with you. Cheerio darling. God bless you and all the luck in the world to you. Au-Revoir.

All my love forever your ever loving wife,
Rene

I LOVE YOU – (in x's)

January 18, 2013

Dear Grama,
I want to start this letter by saying thank you. Thank you for having courage and faith. The decisions that you made in your lifetime have not only shaped your life, but they've

shaped mine. As I sit and read your letter to Papa, 67 years from the day you sat down to write it, I am in complete awe. It's incredible. The love that you and Papa shared was so beautiful. It's the kind of love people dream about.

I feel as if I have been given a gift. The gift of having the letters you wrote to him. I have a glimpse into your life and love that I am truly grateful for. I am taking this gift you have left to me and listening to my heart, which has led me back to the house you wrote these letters from. As I built up the courage and faith you taught me in so many ways, I knocked on the door. The woman who answered, lovingly welcomed me into her home. She listened to my story, asked how she could help and even brought out paper work of the home's history. She let me go into the upstairs bedroom, which I assume was yours. As I looked out the window from that bedroom, I felt like we were sharing something. Sharing a view, lifetimes apart, that was more than just a view. It was connection in its truest form.

After that moment, I now know with every part of me, that I am on the right path. Listening to my heart as I know you did every day of your life. So this is what I will do, Grama. I am here to retrace your steps. I will live here as you did, walk the streets you walked, visit the places you visited and start this journey within a journey. I know you will be with me on this journey in more ways than I am even aware of yet, and I can feel that this experience is going to be more than I ever imagined.

With a granddaughters love & admiration,
Carly

Xoxox

Carly in
front of
Grama's house

Adam and I spent the next few days searching for a flat, or even a room in a flat, with no such luck. In the end, we decided to drop the search as the days started to drop off the calendar. We only had four days left together, and we both decided that we would much rather be enjoying the sites of London than spending our time using the internet in a library somewhere scouring rental ads. Between Elyse and Alec's home in Birmingham and other friends I knew in London, I would work something out. And I remembered hearing Renee say that her daughter was off at college in Alabama, so who knows – maybe I could even stay at my grandmother's old house. It didn't matter. I shrugged off the need to find a place because I just knew that it would all work out.

CHAPTER II

PROPOSAL

The day of Adam's departure was fast approaching, but we were determined to just enjoy every second. We were leaving London the next morning to follow my grandmother's letters for a weekend in Oxford. Sixty-seven years prior, she had made a weekend trip to visit a friend. It had been an incredible week. Between visiting the flat where she lived and meeting Renee and the incredible response to my first blog post, I was on cloud nine. The responses, mostly from family and friends, were so encouraging about this dream I was following. I was overwhelmed with gratitude. But all I wanted to do that night was to put the computer aside and focus on Adam and make the most of what remained of our time together. We talked about the possibility of him staying, but knew we would run out of money fast, and deep down I knew that I needed to do this on my own. I couldn't get over how incredibly supportive and loving he was. How many men would travel to London knowing that they would be leaving their girlfriend there for six months? How many men would be so supportive of what some people saw as a whim or a lovely adventure? He never asked me, "Carly what is the point of this?" Because it was important to me, it was important to Adam.

A huge smile stretched across his face as I leaned over to kiss him. He playfully tickled me to the mattress and started smothering me with kisses until I was out of breath from all of the laughter. As we tucked in nice and close and gave each other an intimate glance, it was almost as if we could physically feel the anticipation of our separation and suddenly clung to one another with intensity. We were gazing into each other's eyes and started to profess our love for one another.

I whispered how happy I was in that moment, in this relationship, and in this life, and he agreed and added, "I know what would make us both even happier. Do you want your birthday present early?" I convincingly explained that since it was past midnight, it was technically already my birthday. As he tucked back in after rifling through his suitcase, he looked me right in the eyes and took my hands. He went on to explain how much he loved me and how he had never felt this kind of love before. He proposed.

I recognized the ring immediately. It was the one I had tried on at the vintage shop next to where I worked in downtown Windsor. My mind flashed back to that day, just a few weeks prior. I had received a call from my best friend Jess, phoning from England, so I stepped out of the shop. He must have bought it then and there.

It was a square solitaire diamond ring with a pinched silver band. It was simple and fit perfectly. I could tell he was nervous because his palms were sweaty and I could feel his heart pounding. It wasn't until the next morning I realized that he hadn't got down on one knee, like most proposals you hear of. He proposed while we were lying in bed, cuddled up nice and close. I guess that was another clue that this life with Adam wouldn't be typical... which I loved. It was the best moment, one that I would never forget.

I didn't sleep a wink that night and couldn't wait to call my mom and Jess. I was calculating the time difference in my head and realized my mom was probably awake in Canada, but I decided to wait. The next morning as I was getting ready, my new ring on my finger kept stopping me dead in my tracks. I would smile and let out a squeal of excitement.

We quickly bid farewell to our rental home in Turnham Green. We were on a bit of a time crunch because of our booked train tickets to Oxford. It had snowed again that morning and had we not been in a rush, I probably would have lingered to take more pictures or make a snowman or two. I settled for tracing a heart in the frosted window and continued on.

As we walked to the nearest train station that we had carefully mapped out the evening before, pre-proposal, we were surprised to see the black steel gate shut tight bearing a note that informed us that the station was closed for weekend maintenance. This, as it turned out, would be one of our first tests as an engaged couple. It was my birthday and our first day being engaged – the last thing we wanted was a travel mishap, the kind that brings out the true colours of someone. Adam was naturally frustrated and determined to figure this out. I, on the other hand, was lost in engagement euphoria. I just wanted things to be easy and, after about two minutes of effort, was ready to give in to a black cab. Adam didn't want to go that route because of the cost and the fact that there were buses running right past us, but it was my birthday and we were engaged and we were in love! Regardless of those magical truths, we continued on in our frustrating mission to find the right bus and walked up and down streets asking one bus driver after the other if we were heading in the right direction toward Marylebone Station.

We finally made it to the station with only a few minutes to spare, which I insisted on using to grab a cup of coffee. Somewhere in the past two years on my own, I had officially become addicted. I loved waking up in the mornings to the sound and smell of coffee brewing. As I noticed the look on Adam's face from the coffee shop queue, I knew I had to be quick. When we finally made it onto the train, we slumped down into the seats and looked at each other and started laughing. It hadn't been an ideal morning, but we had made it through with our love and good humour intact.

Our day in Oxford reclaimed the magic we had hoped for to end our time together in England. We spent the day wandering through Oxford and spent an hour in a pub eating one of my favourite English meals, shepherd's pie, and skyping with our parents using the crappy pub WiFi. Between cutting in and out, we eventually resorted to just holding up my hand with the ring front and center with our smiling faces in the background. We think they got the point. We kissed and giggled and made our way back to the train station to head back to Birmingham. To kill time on the train, we began working on the guest list for our wedding, even though it was a year or more away.

Carly and Adam in Oxford

At this point, we hadn't set a date, but we were running potential dates around. We started dating in May of 2012, so maybe that would be a nice date to set. I knew for sure that I didn't want to be a sweaty bride. Summers in Ontario are usually hot and humid, so I knew I didn't want that. Adam, being a teacher, liked the idea because then he would always be off for our anniversary and we could take trips to places to celebrate, but I wasn't convinced. I love fall – it's my favourite season with all the colours and harvest, crisp cool air and beauty. The fall that I got back from my grand adventure would be quick, but I kind of liked the sounds of that. I wasn't interested in the planning of the fine details that I had seen my friends go through during my 15 weddings in a two-year stage, but I also had a list of about 10 must-haves for the big day. We both knew it would come together in time.

All of the proposal excitement got me thinking of the story of how Papa proposed to Grama. He was on a three-day leave after months of corresponding through letters, and he chose to spend it with her. Papa's voice telling the story played in my head:

"After spending a three day leave with your Grama, she was about to say goodnight and head to bed. It was the perfect moment, so I asked her to marry me. To my surprise, she told me that she had to think about it and was up the stairs and off to bed. Needless to say, I didn't sleep a wink that night. It wasn't until after preparing the morning tea that she came over to the couch that I slept on to say 'Right...darling, about that question....my answer is yes! I would love to marry you.' She made me the happiest man on the planet that day and every single day to follow."

When Adam left just two short days later, I remember not wanting to fall asleep. I was fighting it and trying to savour the feeling of his touch between tears. I missed him already and I was still in his arms. It made me wonder how my grandmother felt when my grandfather returned to Canada with the rest of the troops.

I stood on a chair to watch as he disappeared into the dark, curving streets. There had been another snowfall, and the taxi was unlikely to make it down the side street, so he had to walk to the closest main intersection. I leaned into the cold glass window and stood on my tiptoes on the chair to try and see him again. My heart hurt, my eyes stung, and I was freezing in the cold, dark, empty house without Adam.

I probably stayed there for well over an hour, tiptoed on the chair, when I finally told myself to go to bed. He was gone. I grabbed the phone and calling card and did a quick calculation of the time difference and started calling my people. I got to tell them the exciting news of our engagement, since we decided that would be one thing I would have to look forward to the moment he left that night. After calling the people I wanted to tell personally, I made an announcement online and gladly took the distraction of comments of well wishes and likes.

As my eyes began to fade into much-needed sleep, I wondered how my grandmother did it, 67 years before. How did she say goodbye to her husband of two and a half months and not know for certain when she would see him again, let alone what she would be moving to? Her strength and trust in love helped me sleep that night. Just before I closed my eyes, I broke the silence of the dark room with a tired whisper, "Goodnight, Grama."

The next few days were sad and mopey. What had I done? I was purposely putting us through this challenge. I was choosing this and it didn't feel great in that moment. Luckily, Alec has no time for whining or complaining, so he didn't really give me much sympathy. He did, however, take me for a walk around town and bought me a brownie, then forced me to shower and do my hair. It did feel good to get outside and be part of the world around us. I couldn't mope forever.

That is when I realized that getting myself outside was a quick fix for my sad and missing Adam moods. It was still snowing like a Canadian winter that January, so it sort of eased the blow of home-sickness. My last afternoon walk in Birmingham before I set out for London, I did the loop of the neighbourhood and meandered through the park. The trees were layered with a gorgeous sheet of snow, and I snapped some photos. As I was walking back to the house, I happened to notice a 2p coin in the snow by my boot. That familiar whisper came out again, thanking Grama for showing me she was there.

CHAPTER 12

FINDING A FLAT

I structured my days around my grandmother's letters and started writing to her every so often to share on my blog. A letter that stood out to me was from January 29 1946. As opposed to my experience tracking Adam's flight the moment he left and talking to him over text and video chat, it wasn't until 12 days after saying goodbye to my grandfather that she finally got word that he arrived home safe and sound.

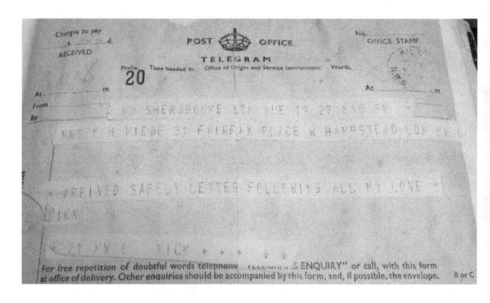

Telegram from Papa

= ARRIVED SAFELY LETTER FOLLOWING ALL MY LOVE = NICK

January 29, 1946

My Darling Nick,
Thanks darling for the telegram I received from you this morn-
ing. I'm very relieved to know that you arrived safely, now I am
waiting patiently for a letter, but it was really lovely to get the
cable darling and I love you all the more for it, if that's possible.
I hope you are still okay as this leaves me but lonely for you. I
'spect you are home by now and that you have started your leave,
boy do I ever wish I was there to help you spend it. Nothing much
has happened around here. I had a letter from Eileen yesterday,
she's also getting fed up and lonely, she's got her cheque from
the pay-master and it was for 8-7-2 (pounds/shilling/pence) so
that's not bad is it? I also got a cheque this morning but I don't
think I'll have to change it yet awhile, I sent Eileen her 3 pounds
I owed her yesterday and I will give Naty his as soon as I see him.
I haven't seen him since you have gone, he has been here twice
but I was out, once I was at Oxford and the other time I was at the
pictures. I might go with Joe to the dog-racing on Saturday as he
was talking about it, Maurice said he might come too, anyway
it would make a change, if I do go I won't take much money so I
can't lose it, would you like to come darling? Do I ever wish you
could. I heard our song again last night on the AFN, I guess that's
the only station they play it now. The papers are still full of the G.I.
brides that sailed in the Argentina on Saturday, it seems a lot of
them have been sea-sick right now I wouldn't mind being sea-
sick if it only meant seeing you at the end. I never thought there
would ever come a time when I would look forward so much to
leave home, I remember when I left home three years ago I was
so home-sick I cried every night for a week, but now I know I shall
only be happy when I am with you once again. You are my family
and my life now. I haven't heard from Danny yet, I gave him my
phone number in case he might like to ring me up. Well darling,
I don't think I have very much more news, everything else is very
much the same, I have been busy all day in the shop, weighing

things up.... I'm still waiting for the sun to shine so as I can take some snaps, maybe it will come out tomorrow... Well darling, I guess that is about all for to-night so I suppose I'd better wash and prepare for bed. By the way darling, you know our black market garage, well in the morning before I get up I lay in bed and I can hear every word that the blokes say, they don't arf make a row too... that's the cockney in me coming out. Well cheerio darling. God Bless You and Good Luck, To the Grandest Husband in all the World. Au-revoir. All my love to you forever.

Your everloving wife,
Rene

I LOVE YOU (in x's)

I booked a train into London for a few days later, even though part of me wanted to stay comfortable and cozy with Elyse and Alec in Birmingham for the whole six months and just do frequent trips into London. The more I thought about it, the more I knew it would never work. I wanted to really do this and get it right, even though I was the one making the rules. Onwards with the flat-search I went. Adam helped me from home and sent me Gumtree links of flats for rent. I'm pretty picky when it comes to a living environment, so only one of the 10 intrigued me because of its fresh coat of white paint and bright coloured canvas print above the fireplace. I sent an email to arrange a viewing.

In an odd twist of fate, my best friend Jess was also living in London at the time and was dating Alec's brother Ollie. They had met two years earlier at Elyse and Alec's wedding in Canada. Ollie came all the way from England for the celebration and let's just say that Ollie and Jess hit it off. Jess and I were roommates in university. We had known each other through friends in high school, but it wasn't until fate had yet again brought us together when the two others we were both hoping to dorm with didn't get into the university we had all applied to. I remember going up to her locker one day and saying, "Hey Jess. I hear you got into Guelph. Want to be my roommate?" The rest, as they say, is history. We became soul sisters that year and have been inseparable ever since.

Knowing I would have Jess and Ollie and Elyse and Alec close by made my decision to move across the pond to pursue the crazy, bold dream of retracing my grandmother's steps a lot easier. I had two of my best friends there to love and support me, and two British brothers who loved me and teased me and treated me like a sister of their own.

I stayed on Jess and Ollie's futon for a night, but realized that wouldn't work for long, so I started looking for temporary living in London. I found a room in a woman's house in Streatham for rent and signed myself up for the week. Jess and Ollie dropped me off there that first night, and I remember feeling a bit nervous and scared. What if this lady is crazy, what if she has a big dog that jumps up on me? Birmingham was looking better by the day.

The homeowner's name was Jane, and she met me at the door with a smile, and sure enough her dog did greet me with a big wet lick to the toes. Ewwww, I thought. After a quick introduction over tea with Jane, she gave me a little tour, and I got myself ready for bed. I missed Adam and felt it quite deeply this time now that I wasn't with Elyse and Alec or Jess and Ollie. It was just me in a strange room with a typically hard-to-read British woman downstairs with her dog.

Finding a flat had turned out to be such a challenge. Maybe, if I was still alive tomorrow, I could just stay here for six months? The room next to mine was big and bright with pretty yellow curtains. Maybe it was available for a long-term rental. The second I smelled the smoke snaking its way up the stairs and into my room I knew it was a no go. I wanted to find a place closer to my grandmother's neighbourhood. A place that wasn't a long bus ride away and that didn't fill with cigarette smoke after I went to bed.

I woke up the next morning and looked out the window. It looked like a scene from *Mary Poppins*. The chimneys on the row houses were a gorgeous contrast to the red brick. The small back-yards that they called gardens, even if there was no actual garden, were seamed together with a wooden fence. The second I looked out the window, I saw a bright red fox walking along the fence. After watching it until it was out of sight, I grabbed my laptop and looked up "symbolism of a fox." The first link to pop up said fortune, luck, and opportunity. I was on the right track.

Ever since I was little, every time we travelled, my dad and I would check out the view of every new place we stayed together. I thought back to the hotel we stayed at on my first trip to England in 1995 with Grama and Papa. My father and I sat at the window of our hotel and watched the double-decker buses and black taxis go by.

Thinking back to that trip brought a flood of memories to my mind. Getting my first Spice-Girls inspired platform shoes, meeting Grama's family members, posing in front of the guards at the Tower of London as I wore my favourite overall jeans and crop top, and being embarrassed by my Uncle Roger pulling his pants down in a restaurant after spilling hot tea on his lap. There was never a dull moment with my family, especially my mom's side. Looking back, we were so lucky that we went when we did, because three years later my grandmother passed away. I was so grateful that I got to experience Grama's beloved city with her and that she got to show it off to us once and for all.

London
1995

That morning, I took a bus to see the flat in Willesden Green with the fresh coat of white paint. I loved it immediately. It was two tube stops away from my grandmother's neighbourhood and within a short walk to the tube. It needed a little bit of character, despite the lovely print hanging over the fireplace. But that could be easily fixed with the addition of a colourful duvet and some fresh flowers. I signed the lease agreement and moved in the following week.

That weekend, I went back to Birmingham to spend time with Elyse and Alec and gather all the things I had left with them until I found a more permanent place. I took advantage of their speedy WiFi to reach out to a few local groups online to ask for hidden gems in my grandmother's neighbourhood and to tell them my story. I had no idea as I was crafting those inquiries to find places to go and sights to see that I was creating an opportunity for taking my story public. Overnight, my blog had 2,000 visits. The next day, I got an email from a gal working for an ancestry website expressing interest in making a short video about my story. *Yes! Sure! I'd love to!* was my response. As I was saying goodbye to Elyse and Alec, she joked, "Call me if *BBC Breakfast* calls because I'm totally coming with you!"

CHAPTER 13

MEDIA FRENZY

I barely had time to settle into my new flat before I was heading out for my video shoot with the ancestry website. When they contacted me, they were working on an "Every Family Has a Story" campaign, and they wanted to use the story of me following my grandmother's letters as part of their advertising drive. I was excited they were interested.

I was nervous on the way there, but I calmed down when I got to the house where we filmed. At this point, Google Maps had become my constant companion, mapping out exactly how I could get from point A to point B. I took two tube lines that morning and then a quick walk from Oval Station to the gorgeous Victorian row homes with street level walk-ups. It was the British version of Carrie Bradshaw's NYC brownstone.

I was greeted by a team of four and immediately felt at home in the cozy living room setup. The house belonged to a friend of a crewmember, and there were books, instruments, a cozy fireplace, and bay windows. A rocker, a trunk, and antique furniture decorated the room. They gave me water and a granola bar and offered me fruit. The crew had sent me a rundown of how the filming would go, which they reviewed upon my arrival.

The shoot took five hours. The camera and sound person was a woman named Heather from NYC who put me at ease the moment we started. She told me to just tell her a story and not to worry about the camera. It wasn't live, so they could always cut footage that didn't fit. We talked, then cut, then were rolling again. They were asking me questions and prompting me, so it felt like an interview that they would eventually make one-sided.

After the inside shots and footage were taken, they brought me outside to get some shots walking around London. They had me walk up and down the street, up the stairs to the house, knock on the door, and then walk through a park. Being followed by a camera crew was quite the experience. It sure did turn heads, and I tossed my phone at one of the crewmembers to take an action shot of what was happening. For a moment, I felt like I was looking in on someone else's life. I couldn't believe how fast this all happened. It still felt surreal to me.

After the shoot, I had dinner with Jess in my new neighbourhood pub. Jess and Ollie lived in South London, about 45 minutes away on the tube. We ordered a bottle of wine and some dinner, as I filled her in on my glamorous day.

On the way home, I stopped by at the movie store. *Letters to Juliette* was on sale so I picked it up. When the movie first came out, I watched it six times back-to-back. There was something about the story that spoke to me; I suppose it was my connection to letters.

Tucked away in my flat in London, I watched *Letters to Juliette* again. I felt like I was seeing the movie for the first time. I was beginning to see what precious objects letters were. They carry the energy of the past into the present, along with the hopes and wishes of the people who wrote them. They can, like my grandmother's letters did, sit dormant for years and once found, take on a whole new meaning.

The next morning, I followed Grama's letters to the Odeon. I assumed it was the one closest to her house, the Swiss Cottage Odeon Theatre that still stood. When I walked in, I interrupted three young staff members behind the concession stand who were taking a break from the crowds between showings. My days of working at my hometown theatre with two of my best friends flashed through my mind. We did the exact same thing. You could only restock candy and clean up fallen popcorn for so long. I explained why I was there, and they smiled and seemed vaguely interested. I asked if they had any pictures of the theatre from the 1940s. To my surprise, they gave me four canvas prints that were "taking up space and collecting dust."

When I got back to my flat later that day, I met my flatmates. I shared the space with three other people. I had my own room, but we shared a bathroom and the kitchen.

There was the very sweet 70-year-old man from Afghanistan who spoke broken English. After a few weeks, I began finding gifts of fruit in my cupboard in the kitchen. He left apples, oranges, pears, and grapes. It was like having a kind grandpa or older uncle close by. I shared my adventures around London, and he taught me to cook Afghani food. One night, he pulled out an atlas to show me where he was from, and I showed him where I lived in Canada. When I thought about leaving, I thought we would become pen pals, exchanging letters between the flat in London and my home in Canada. But evidently, he had been entertaining different fantasies. One night right before I moved out of the flat, he came into my room and tried to kiss me. I pushed him out of the doorway and locked the door. I was stunned and then upset and then I laughed.

He was old enough to be my grandfather! I warned Sophia who had the room down the hall to be careful – Uncle was *not* who we thought he was.

Sophia was a theatre student from Germany. She had short hair, wore little makeup, and had the kind of unique beauty that had people coming up to her asking if she ever considered runway modeling before. That was not her kind of thing. She preferred literature, going to plays, and deep conversation. We became quick friends. Sophia invited me to go to plays with her, and I invited her on walks in the park. Strolling around London, we talked about the challenges our generation faces with social media, we talked about my book, her plays, creative expression, and writing. We talked about London, world travel, family, and legacy. I felt like I could talk to her for hours about everything under the sun. We had a special bond.

And then there was the guy from India who stayed awake all night trading on the stock exchange. I only saw this man of mystery a handful of times in the six months I lived in the flat.

We were on the second floor of a building above a cell phone shop. The stairs led up to a long hallway with bedroom doors. There wasn't a common area, but Sophia and I would sometimes visit and hang out in each other's rooms. Her room was a little bit bigger and had a sink, large fridge, small burner, and room for a table and chairs. Other than that, it was just a hallway with four rooms, a kitchen, and a bathroom.

Because of our different routines and schedules, we rarely ran into problems with sharing. I would make breakfast in the kitchen, but eat it in my room at my desk while checking Facebook and my blog. I had my own mini fridge, so it was easy to keep to myself when I wanted to. It was next to a Sainsbury grocery store, which came in quite handy for groceries and the 2-pound tulip special.

I loved my little flat, despite its size. It was perfect for me and was really all that I could afford. It was the same price as my entire two-bedroom apartment back in Windsor, but this was London, and I was happy.

After the ancestry video was posted, chaos broke out around my story. A producer from *BBC Breakfast* called and asked if I would consider doing an interview. I immediately called Elyse to tell her the crazy news, and she quickly made arrangements to take time off work to be there.

Then, *The Mail Online* called and *The Times* and *The Daily Mirror*, followed by *BBC Radio*. My room in the flat was littered with contracts, notes, and stacks of Post-Its I used to keep track of the appearances, interviews, and phone calls. I was totally unprepared for all of the attention, but I loved that my grandmother's story was resonating with so many people.

Elyse met me in Manchester, for the *BBC Breakfast* interview. I took the train from London to Manchester and she came up from Birmingham. The second I stepped out of the taxi to catch the train, I noticed a coin by my boot. Thanks for the nudge, Grama. The network arranged for me to stay at a hotel close to the studio. My room was beautiful with two queen-size beds, a huge desk, and a modern, shiny bathroom that put my shared bathroom to shame. Before Elyse arrived, I opened the window to look at the view. It looked out onto an outdoor courtyard and another hotel twice the size. Then I did something I rarely do: I opened the Bible to the Book of Ruth. I could feel my nerves getting the better of me, and the room seemed awfully quiet. I needed some comfort, distraction, and anything that would take my mind back to Grama and the purpose of why I was here. I had remembered my mom telling me that my grandmother's funeral service was based around passages from the Book of Ruth. It was a story quite similar to hers. She embarked to a new land, into a new family, leaving behind all that she knew, accepting it as her own.

I read the lines carefully, "Where you go I will go, and where you stay I will stay. Your people will be my people and your God my God." I silently thanked her for her courage and decided to follow suit.

We got up the next morning quite early. I wanted to straighten my hair, even though they told me someone would do my hair and makeup. The show aired at 7 a.m. sharp, and I would likely be called on around 7:40. Just as we were about to leave for the studio, I made Elyse switch clothes with me. She was always the more fashionable of the two of us, and her outfit was more sophisticated than mine. Elyse didn't hesitate – she stripped off her black blazer and pretty fashion jewelry and handed them to me. She wanted me to look and feel good like true friends do.

BBC Breakfast couches with Elyse

The interview went great. I was surprised how easy it was to answer questions with a TV camera staring at me that I knew was beaming my face out to millions of people drinking their morning coffee. After the interview, the producer and Elyse congratulated me on how well I had done.

Just like everything though, there's always so much more to the story behind the scenes. Because a PR agency was involved, there were a few expectations put on me to mention the names of a few organizations. The truth was reporters are trained to ask questions to veer you away from any type of promotion or advertisement on air. And let's be serious, I was just trying to keep my cool and remember *my own* name, let alone anyone else's.

Being the people pleasing person that I was, I worried for the entire train ride back to London that I had ruffled feathers, disappointed people, and let people down. I felt naïve and in over my head, and I was overwhelmed. I had to work really hard to keep shifting the focus back to the amazing experience I just had and tried to stay positive.

A few days after the BBC show aired, I got a call from a literary agent named Jacob. I didn't have a clue what a literary agent even was. I met him a few days later. His agency was housed in a four-story brick building in Holborn. He answered all of my questions with mild amusement – what does a literary agent do exactly? What is a proposal? Despite all of my ignorance about publishing and writing and agents, he sent me a contract for representation. Because of my overwhelm with letting people down, I was too scared to sign anything at the time. I decided to wait until the end of the journey to think about writing a book. I needed to live it first.

February 14, 1946

My Darling Nick,
My Darling Valentine. First of all I love you and miss you terribly,
if they don't soon hurry things up I shall soon start and try to walk
the Atlantic, do you think it would take me very long darling?
Don't mind that little out burst. I just had to say it, but I mean
every word from the bottom of my heart. Now I must thank you
for the two lovely letters I got this morning, the ones you wrote
on the boat. It was sweet of you to write it darling and I enjoyed
every word and every minute it took reading it, and by the way
I have been reading it again all day long, all twenty-five pag-
es!! It didn't take long to get here did it darling, only about two
weeks, let's hope everything gets done in record time like that. I
also got another air-mail letter from you this afternoon, if they
keep coming like that I shan't grumble, the only thing that could
make me much, much, much happier is when I am with you once
again for ever, please God. Well darling, your little wifey has been
up to her favourite vice again, Joe persuaded me to go dog-racing
again tonight so I did, but this time I won five pounds, I wish you
were here to help me spend it. I must tell you how it happened, I
was about even just before the last race when I noticed a dog was
going to run who was called thirty days so I thought ah! thirtieth
of October (but you wouldn't remember that date, would you?)
anyway I chose him three times and it won lovely so I came away
five pounds better off. Of course I nearly died of heart failure at the
end because it was such a close finish. They had to have a photo
finish but they had to say it won in the end. Oh! I'm a fool and a
chatter-box, here I have rambled on all about myself and I ha-
ven't asked you how you are darling. I hope you are okay as this
leaves me but as you can see very excited, but I suppose you know
by now that you have a very excitable wife, I don't know how I
am going to come over all in one piece, I shall probably come with
odd clothes on or something like that, but don't worry darling,
Mum will never persuade me not to come, my place is with you

*wherever you are. Of course, my excitement at coming is mixed
with regret at leaving everyone, but I guess that is only natural.
It is now half-past twelve and I am sitting up in our bed writing this, everyone else is asleep but I couldn't go to sleep without
writing to you. I'm sitting here thinking wouldn't it be heavenly
if I could just turn to you at my side and kiss you and love you all
to pieces. Well dearest I guess this is where I sign off. Good-night
darling, God Bless You and pleasant dreams.
Au-revoir.
All my love to you forever, your ever loving wife,
Rene*

I LOVE YOU (in x's)

February 14 2013

My Darling Valentine & Fiance,
Will you be mine, forever? I love you so much, Adam. You
mean the world to me. I had quite a memorable Valentine's
Day on the BBC Breakfast Show and BBC Radio. It was a
day that I will remember forever and will go down in the
books, in MY book, as one of the best days of my life. It
was absolutely a Top 5 moment, up there with the day you
proposed (obviously not as amazing, though). The studio
was a bright, creative space and everyone was so nice. I was
on T.V. in front of 7 million viewers, babe! It was scary,
amazing, exciting, overwhelming and out of this world. I
wish, with every bone in my body, that you could have been
there to experience it all with me. The green room, makeup,
lights, camera, ACTION! It was an incredible feeling and I
felt just a little bit of pressure...okay, maybe a lot of pressure. I had to focus on getting words out of my mouth,
making sense, being present, and not running out of the
room due to the nerves that happen when you put your life,

goals and dreams in public like that. I did my best and I did pretty darn good, if I do say so myself. The hosts were so welcoming and made me feel very comfortable. Charlie gave me quite a nice compliment. He said that it is a very nice story and that I tell it so charmingly. My mantra for the day was "Remembering Rene" and I had to use it on many occasions: when my heart was pounding so hard that I could barely hear my thoughts, to quiet my thoughts once I could hear them and when I got sidetracked by the cameras, prompts and British celebrity hosts in front of me. It worked and it reminded me about what this media craze is all about. It's the human interest in what I'm really doing here. I'm honouring those before me and realizing the sacrifices they made 67 years ago all in the name of love. Speaking of love, I love you to the moon and back. You make me so happy and even though this adventure is more than I ever dreamed it would be after only one month, I am excited for the day that we will be together again. Gleefully planning our wedding day, dreaming up what married life will be like, buying our first home, planning lovely vacations together and perhaps the most exciting of all, talking about creating a family together. The thought of passing this journey on to our children, warms my heart. I can't help but think about my Grama and Papa in 1946 dreaming about this kind of stuff, too.

With all my love on Valentine's Day,
Carly

I LOVE YOU (in x's)

CHAPTER 14

MOTHERS & DAUGHTERS

After the flurry of media attention, I energetically crashed. I had several crappy days that just blended into the next. I was very aware that I was on this fabulous, once-in-a-lifetime journey and that I was incredibly grateful for being in London, but at the same time, felt a little derailed by all of the excitement and whirlwind of the past month. My story going as public as it did as quickly as it did felt like a lot of pressure. The self-doubt was real. I started to wonder if I had what it takes to write a book, as I had been saying since day one. I felt like there were a lot more sets of eyes on me now and, of course, there were the dreaded comment sections of news articles telling me all sorts of things. Like most people, even though there were 100 people saying beautiful lovely things, the negative ones seemed to play on repeat in my mind.

For the first time ever, I was responsible for my own schedule. I was completely the boss of my time. Only I would know or care if I followed my grandmother's letters or spent the week in my bathrobe, with my laptop propped up next to me bingeing on reruns of "Sex and the City". Like so many other bloggers and writers, there were a few days where I felt stuck. I felt as if I couldn't move forward or didn't have the energy to research and find the places my grandmother spoke about in her letter. There were days when I didn't want to get dressed and go out into the world in hopes that my day would be interesting enough to write about. Thankfully, days like those were rare, and I quickly figured out ways to shake them off.

On one particular uninspiring day, I remembered to connect to Grama and decided to do some research on Canadian war brides and found CBC clips of war bride reunions throughout the years. I was watching a news clip from war brides in 1986, who went back to retrace the journey their husbands made liberating country after country and to visit London again. As the camera scanned the crowd of the excited brides, some returning back to England for the first time in 40 years, there was my grandmother! Right at the front of the line, shaking hands with the mayor, with the biggest smile on her face. There was even a clip of my grandfather carrying the bags behind her, and his grin was bigger than hers. I realized watching the footage that I was truly following in my grandmother's footsteps, embarking on a journey across the ocean, having my own CBC interview as well, and waiting for my time to be up here in London so I too could return to the man I love. I wondered what my grandmother would think about it all.

I wondered if she would have asked me what the hell I was thinking. She had to be separated from my grandfather. I was choosing to be separated from Adam. I missed him. I missed my family, and I missed my friends. Part of me wanted to go home. So I did what many mature adults do when they can't decide what to do: I called my mom.

My mom has always been my biggest fan. She always knows how to remind me to breathe and that Grama would probably want me to try my best to keep calm and carry on. She has also always expected the unexpected from me. Going to Korea, investing in coach training, and embarking on this trip, none of it surprised her. She has been married to a creative impulsive for three decades so she gets me. When my dad is trying to write a song, he often has to walk away from his guitar altogether. Sometimes even for two or three days, until the words and music come to him, naturally and unforced. They both encouraged me to get away from my computer and out of my head. To take a break from writing and go do something, anything but continue to stare at the four walls of my room.

It was late so I decided to take their advice first thing the next day. I ended the night watching a movie my grandmother had written about *Wonder Man*. It was quite entertaining, and I loved seeing the cars and the fashions that my grandmother would have seen driving around and worn. I set my alarm for bright and early the next morning.

When I woke up, I was determined to get outside and move around. I went straight to my grandmother's neighbourhood and walked by her old house. The old fashioned lamp posts and converted stable houses made it easy to picture what the street looked like when she walked there in 1946. I went to a coffee shop around the corner from her house, journal in hand, and sat on the patio to feel the warmth of the sun. I told myself to go back to the basics of writing: write about what I hear, feel, and see. I was forcing myself to write when a mother pushing a stroller with a little girl passed by. I smiled at the child and rather than smile back, she stuck her tongue out at me. It was just what I needed. I felt as if the universe was sending me a message through her. "Hey, you. Yeah, you. The girl who calls herself a writer. Seriously, loosen up!"

And I did. I started to see and hear things differently. When I got out of my own way, I could hear the sound of the Italian girl-friends chatting and laughing as if they were the only two people for miles. I heard the hiss of the steam forcing its way from the espresso machine inside the shop, and I heard the tapping of heels hurrying down the sidewalk. A man hummed a chipper tune. Suddenly, there was so much to write about and so much going on in the world around me that once I started, I wanted to capture every detail.

When I got back to my flat, I walked in to the best surprise. It was a huge parcel from Adam and after running up the stairs and plopping myself on my bed to tear it open, I discovered that it was filled with close to 50 notes and letters. He had contacted one of my co-workers and had them draft up love letters and notes. He got both sides of our families involved and about 20 friends. He knew that the media frenzy took me by storm, so had arranged this big package filled to the brim with love, encouragement, and support. It made me feel so special. I spent the entire night reading and re-reading the thoughtful words from my loved ones and was surprised at how connected I felt to all of them after just seeing their handwriting and reading their words. I felt their love and support in every single line.

I also had an email from Renee, the woman who was living in my grandmother's house. She had been talking to some of the neighbours about my story, and she found a woman who had lived in the neighbourhood since the 40s. All of a sudden, I had plans for the next day. I would start knocking on more doors and continue to tell my story to see what nuggets of gold I could uncover.

It wasn't long until the idea started floating around that perhaps a visit from my mom would help me get back on track after the whirlwind that I just experienced. All it had taken to get her here was a "you-have-to-do-this" and a "this-opportunity-may-not-come-around-again" nudge from my dad and the flight was booked. She was my strongest link to my grandmother and having her visit was a huge gift. It was just like her to want to swoop in to remind me what my time here was all about. And to get to explore London and be part of the journey for a few weeks...why not?

Carly and her mom at Piccadilly Circus

As I waited to meet her at London Bridge Station off the train that comes direct from the airport, a flood of memories came to my mind of all the times she came to the rescue. She was the rock of the family, the solid one. I was forever calling her in a panic about a university paper that was due the next morning that I would surely never finish or this boy problem or that. We were very close, and we both felt blessed to have the relationship that we did. And only occasionally, when things, or rather I, got too out of hand, spiraling from crisis to crying to asking how I would possibly get through this, would she have to lovingly put me in my place. She'd tell me to get a grip, calm down, and to breathe.

The moment I saw her bright red, curly hair in the sea of Monday morning commuters in their business suits, I felt a wave of comfort that only being with my momma brings. It felt so nice to be in her arms, even though in reality, I had towered over her since I was 17. I secretly loved that my chin could land right on top of her curls and that she could tuck in for a hug that was equally as comforting for me as it was her. I was here for her, too. We were more than just mother and daughter – we were friends.

Adam and I had just set the date for our wedding for May 24, 2014. After throwing a few ideas on the table, like Adam and our immediate families coming over to England to get married where my grandparents had years earlier, we decided that it was unrealistic and way too expensive to arrange. My loan was already dwindling as it was, so we set a date for the following spring, which would give us a chance to plan together, start saving, and get some help with the details from family and friends. The date also seemed fitting, as it had been the date that we made our relationship official back in 2012, and it was Adam's parents' wedding anniversary. We could honour the legacy of love on the Verheyen side. That made me excited to think about it.

I was pleasantly surprised that I actually had any interest in the wedding planning at all. I knew my must-haves and surprisingly had some opinions on certain details of the day. We started a shared Pinterest board so that we could run fun ideas by one another and brainstorm our thoughts. One thing that we decided was to have a big engagement party right after I returned from England to celebrate my being home and the engagement with our friends and family. He and Mom were handling all the details since all I could do from London was give them a thumbs up or down. Since my 27 *Dresses* days, I had taken quite a few notes. The simpler the better was my motto.

Mom and I spent our first day together browsing the shops for a dress for the engagement party. Having been in the 40s mindset already with the letters, I wanted to stick with the vintage theme, so we decided to check out Camden Market. I gathered up a few dresses and headed to the fitting room. I was trying the first dress on when I looked down and noticed a shiny coin at my feet. Grama was there, just as she had been the morning after Adam and I got engaged. I picked it up and dropped it in my purse. I would add it to my growing collection of Grama's coins. I took it as a nudge from Grama and bought the dress. It was a short, cream, A-line dress made with lace. It was a classic babydoll dress. It made me feel cute, and for an engagement party, it was perfect.

Mom and I had talked about the type of wedding dress shop we had hoped to find. We meandered up and down streets, hoping we would stumble upon the perfect bridal boutique. We stopped for a photo op on the corner of Islington High Street and Camden Passage and there it was! Exactly the way we pictured it. Tucked away on a quaint side street lined with cafés, bistros, boutiques, and specialty shops. As I stood there looking in, with my hands held together as if I was already holding my bouquet, I said, "It's beautiful! Look at that dress, Mom." We must have been standing there staring into the shop for quite a while, because the shop owner finally motioned us to come in, despite the CLOSED FOR FITTING sign on the door. We made an appointment to go back later in the week, and we could hardly contain how excited we were.

When we were at dinner that evening, I pulled one of Grama's letters from my purse, and Mom and I read it together.

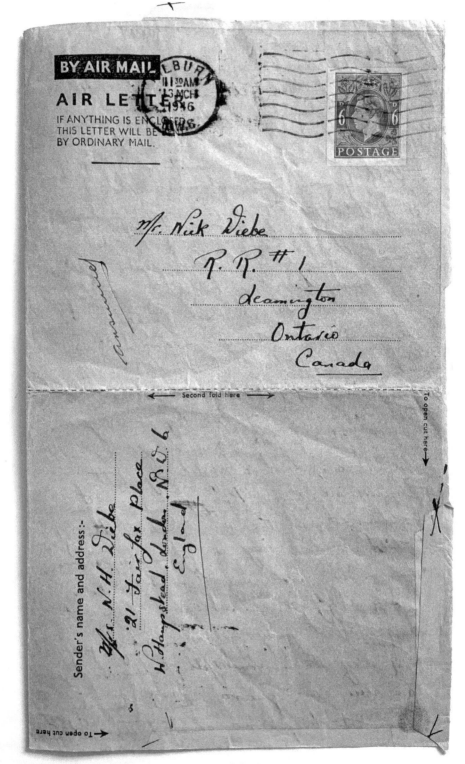

BY AIR MAIL

AIR LETTER

IF ANYTHING IS ENCLOSED
THIS LETTER WILL BE SENT
BY ORDINARY MAIL.

6 POSTAGE 6

Mr. Nick Wiebe
R. R. # 1,
Leamington
Ontario
Canada

← Second fold here →

To open cut here→

Sender's name and address:-
Mrs. N. H. Wiebe
21 Fairfax Place
W. Hampstead. London. N.W. 6
England

←To open cut here→

92

My Darling, Here I am once again on the wrong side of the Atlantic. No letter from you to-day but I would have been surprised if there was one as it is Tuesday. I hope you are okay, darling as this leaves me but missing and longing for you terribly. Everything back here is very much the same, the usual routine. I have just written to Albert, its his birthday to-day he is now 23, I can't imagine it because he always seemed to me my kid brother but he would murder me if he heard me call him that now. I expect by now you are demobbed, darling and you are now a civilian, I done right by letting the bureau know that you were discharged on the 5th March although I told a lie by a few days as she said yesterday that it makes a big difference. Now I have the feeling that I may get my sailing papers any day, its a wonderful feeling darling as you can guess and its the only thing that keeps me cheerful these days.

But the trouble is that one day my
hopes get raised and then the next
day I think it may be months before I
do come over, but never mind darling
one day, please God, we will be to-gether
~~parted~~ for ever never to be parted
again. I didn't do much at work
to-day, except ~~cou~~ counting points, another
customer gave me a present to-day, a
belt, I do alright don't I? I meant to
tell you this before but I forgot, Joe
made me laugh ever so much on
Sunday, we were having tea and I
said I had better not pour out of the
teapot after you Joe as I might get
twins so he said yes do and call them
Willie & Winnie he is crackers isn't
he? but it queers it runs in our family
don't you dare say yes. Phoebe is going
to buy me a cookery book, don't laugh
and I am really going to study the
art. Elsie has just been up here
telling Lency and me all her troubles,
she started talking about ten and its
now half-past eleven, thats women for
you, still I queers when men start
they are just as bad. Do you know
darling I was just thinking I haven't had a

94

had a drink since you have gone, don't you think I am good? But you know, ever since that night I got gin-soaked I guess I have got gone off drink. Well darling I guess thats about all the news for to-night. I tasted something I havn't had for six years to-day, my Aunt brought Mum a banana to-day so we all had a bite each, I wished too while I was eating it, I bet you can guess what I wished. All I can think of to say now darling is that I love you and long to see you terribly, at the end of each day I am happy because its one day nearer to you, P.G.E. Cheerio darling, Good-night, God Bless You and may all your dreams be pleasant ones, Good-luck Au-revoir

All my love to you forever
your everloving wifey
Rene

x x

March 12 1946

My Darling,
Here I am once again on the wrong side of the Atlantic. No letter from you today but I would have been surprised if there was one as it is Tuesday. I hope you are okay, darling as this leaves me but missing and longing for you terribly. Everything back here is very much the same, the usual routine. I have just written to Albert. It's his birthday today he's now 23, I can't imagine it because he always seems to me, my kid brother but he would murder me if he heard me call him that now. I expect by now, you are demobbed darling and you are now a civilian, I done right by letting the bureau know that you were discharged on the 5th of March, although I told a lie by a few days as she said yesterday that it makes a big difference. Now I have the feeling that I may get my sailing papers any day, it's a wonderful feeling darling as you can guess and it's the only thing that keeps me cheerful these days. But the trouble is that one day my hopes get raised and then the next day I think it may be months before I do come over, but never mind darling one day, please God, we will be together forever never to be parted again. I didn't do much at work today except counting points. Another customer gave me a present today, a belt, I do alright don't I? I meant to tell you this before but I forgot, Joe made me laugh ever so much on Sunday. We were having tea and I said "I better not pour out of the teapot after you, Joe as I might get twins" so he said "Yes, do and call them Willie & Winnie," he is crackers isn't he? But I guess it runs in our family, don't you dare say yes. Phoebe is going to buy me a cookery book, don't laugh, and I'm really going to study the art. Elsie has just been up here telling Janey and me all her troubles, she started talking about 10 and it's now half past 11, that's women for you, still I guess when men start they are just as bad. Do you know darling I was just thinking I haven't had a drink since you have gone, don't you think I am good? But you know ever since that night I got gin soaked I guess I have gone off drink. Well darling I guess that's about all the news for to-

night. I tasted something I haven't had for 6 years today, my aunt brought mum a banana today so we all had a bite each, I wished too while I was eating it, I'll bet you can guess what I wished. All I can think of to say now darling is that I love you and long to see you terribly, at the end of each day I am happy because it's one day nearer to you. Please God. Cheerio darling, Good-night, God-Bless you and may all your dreams be pleasant ones. Good-Luck. Au-revoir. All my love to you forever.

Your everloving wifey,

Rene

I LOVE YOU DARLING (in x's)

We marveled at how much life she packed into the letter and into her time in England. I had mentioned the letter to my mom the week before when we talked on the phone, telling her about Grama's joy at eating a banana for the first time after the war ended. She had emailed me that evening.

Carly,

I feel like I have to write to you. I have been thinking a lot about what you learned today about Grama sharing the sweet taste of a banana with her family after a 6-year ration. I can't even imagine. It really illustrates how tough things were back then, but it also got me thinking about their life together and how they came to Canada with no jobs, little money, but lots of love. They built a life together, made a very successful living, saved for a fun retirement and were able to buy a vacation home in Florida and travel the world. What a dream...and that's where you are today. Full of unknowns, but the one sure thing is your love for Adam. Don't you see, that's all you need. I know you see it, but sometimes we get distracted by our modern world, and our self-doubt. So my love, you have been given a rare gift, a "time machine" in the words of a good friend. Use that machine, treasure every day, and know that when you are back with those you love, it will be like that sweet taste of a forbidden fruit.

Love always,
Mom

On the way back to the flat after a day of wedding day dreaming, we stopped at a shop to make one last purchase. As we read Grama's letter together again, we shared the sweet taste of a banana. And we both made a wish. Mine was for more of this. More connection. More love. More life.

My mom and I made some wonderful memories going for high tea at the Ritz, traipsing around the city exploring the sights, visiting pubs, and showing her all of the magical places I had found from retracing Grama's letters. The truth was, though, having my mom there wasn't all roses and sunshine. Having her share my small room was not easy and created a slight role reversal for us. She was in my space, using my things, and suddenly I was the one telling her to hang her towel up and to be sure to use her own towel, not mine. I complained and rolled my eyes and reverted to my bratty 16-year-old self when she didn't respond the way I wanted. When she looked at me in confusion over what towel was hers, I stormed over to my desk, the whole two steps that it took me, and grabbed a black marker. I promptly wrote my name on the tag of my towel, shaking my head as an irritated mother would do. "It's really not that hard to keep track of what towel is yours and where you hang it in this 100-square-foot room, Mom," I said in annoyance.

We always found a way to brush these sort of moments off and move on though, especially with such exciting things on the horizon. My wedding dress appointment rolled around, and mom and I headed over. "I just think that it's so special that we're looking for your dress in London!" my mom said sentimentally on the tube. "I just know Grama would have been thrilled."

By the time we reached the shop, we couldn't contain how excited we were. Genevieve was the consultant of my dreams. She was a hopeless romantic and loved the fine details of a couple's love story. She asked me what kind of wedding we planned to have and was curious about what brought me to London. She was fascinated by the letters that guided me here and absolutely adored my project. Her personal easy style made me feel very relaxed. Mom and I had the whole fitting area to ourselves. Genevieve narrowed down the 10 dresses that I chose and brought out six that were in my budget, and I began trying them on. It felt like a Goldilocks moment. My reaction to dress one, which was a vintage-looking mermaid-style with a lace overlay, was "Oh, this is nice!" To dress two, the gorgeous and simple satin gown, I said, "Oh, I like this!" But dress number three, the flowing A-line dress with straps with a boho relaxed feel got an "I LOOOOOVE this!" I continued trying others on, but kept glancing over at dress three, and just knew that it was my dress. They didn't have my size, so they ordered it. It was set to arrive in a few months.

The highlight of my mom's visit was by far reconnecting with some of my grandma's relatives. People my mother and I had briefly met on our trip to London in 1995 when my grandmother was alive. The only other time my mom had met them was on her visit over to England with my grandmother in 1973. Before coming to London this time, Mom reached out to some family members, and she heard back right away from Grama's niece Pauline, the daughter of Grama's brother Joe and his wife Phoebe.

Before we met them, I was leafing through the letters and noticed there were two letters dated on the 18, one from my grandmother and one from Phoebe. When I showed it to mom, her eyes lit up: "We are meeting Phoebe's daughter tomorrow." And I knew this was yet another of the special meetings my grandmother seemed to keep arranging for me on this trip.

The instant we saw Pauline, Mom and I felt like my grandmother was there with us. It was eerie really. Her mannerisms and her laughter were just like my grandmother's. Pauline told us about her memories of Grama and Papa getting married. She was 9 at the time. She fondly recalled how my grandmother came over to her parent's house to play cards in the long months she spent waiting to get her papers so she could finally be reunited with my grandfather. She told us what uncertain times those were. They had no idea what tomorrow would bring, but despite the worry and concern that permeated everything, my grandmother had a way of letting loose, having fun, and sharing a laugh that made everyone feel like it would be okay. Pauline also talked about how honoured she had been that my grandmother had travelled all the way from Canada in 1955 for her wedding.

I gave Pauline and her daughter a copy of the letter her mother wrote to my grandfather. They loved seeing her mother's handwriting. That day was such a gift for all of us. We laughed, shared stories, asked questions, and for a few hours felt like a whole family again.

When mom hugged Pauline goodbye, she had a hard time letting her go. It was like being hugged by her mom, a feeling she hadn't had in a long time. I was overwhelmed with love, gratitude, and joy for these women, those here and those who lived in our memories. I had been living this quest for almost a year now, mentally, emotionally, and for the past two months, physically. On that day, in those moments shared with Pauline and her daughter, I felt connected. I felt like I was home.

After saying a heartfelt goodbye to Pauline and her daughter, I found myself in the dress aisle of a department store in a heap of tears. I was overwhelmed with emotion. As she smoothed my hair and patted my back, Mom said the perfect thing: "Today brought back sweet memories of my mom – the best times with my mom and her spirit was alive in that pub today."

March 25, 1946

My Darling,
Many thanks for the three smashing letters I got from you today,
darling. I hope you are quite okay as this leaves me but just long-
ing for you. Everything back here is very much the same, still no
sailing papers but I guess we haven't waited long enough but it
sure is hard waiting, but I guess it's true what they say all good
things come to those that wait do you think so darling? Janey
and I have just gone mad and moved all the furniture around,
you know me for moving furniture, when we get together I guess
you'll never know from one day to the other where everything is
going to be, just your crazy little wife darling. How is the work go-
ing darling? I hope they are not working you too hard, and I wish
from the bottom of my heart that I was there to console you in the
evenings when you come home. It sure does seem a waste for me
to be over here but I guess all we can do is blame the Canadian
Government. I think the cooker being gas is wonderful darling as
that is what I am used to, I just wondered what it was. Talking
about that night and us frying the chips, Jane and I were doing
another bill of remembering the other night and we were think-
ing about that afternoon when you and Bob came in from the Brit.
One afternoon late and we pretended to be cross with you and
you brought ices and they were on the table melting, do you re-
member darling, it took all my time to stop myself bursting out
laughing. By the way darling next time I see you remind me to
be cross with you (some hopes), so you think if you had put on
the charm (Casanova) you would have got what you wanted, well
darling what a pity you didn't try, oh! Yeah, something tells me I
wouldn't be Mrs. Wiebe now if you had. Seriously though darling,
I know you wouldn't have because we were just made for each
other and to wait, looks like we do nothing else but, and we are
married now. It's been a real lovely day over here too to-day, real
lovely Spring weather but my Spring and Summer will start when
I am with my darling husband. Guy Lombardo was on the wire-

less to-night so I brushed up my dancing (with Dixie) just to see if I had forgotten anything, Mum thought I had gone mad. Then he played our song so I just had to sit down and listen, and boy did he ever make me feel a little on the lonely side. Well darling, I guess that's about all the news for tonight except that I love you, miss you and long for you terribly but you know that don't you darling? I think the next person who asks me when I am going I'll throw something at them, did I say that, gee! I sound tough don't I? Well darling, I guess now I'll go into bed and dream of you. Good-night darling, God Bless You and may all your dreams be pleasant ones, Good Luck Sweetheart, Au-revoir. All my love to you forever.
Your everloving wifey.
Rene

I LOVE YOU Always Darling (in x's)

March 25, 2013

Dear Grama,

Mom has gone home today and as I reflect back on what a gift the past 2 weeks have been, I feel grateful. It was absolutely wonderful having her here with me, on this journey within your journey.

It dawned on me a few nights ago that this might be the last mother daughter trip we ever have together, just the two of us. My mother and I have wonderful memories together. In 2003, after my first set of university exams, she took me on a long, dreamt-about trip to New York City. For as long as I can remember, I had a fascination with the lights and wonder of that great city. It was our first mother daughter trip and the bond and memories made on that trip will last forever.

Our second trip was when she came for a visit when I was living in Korea in 2008. I had been there for three months, and when she mentioned coming to visit, I was beyond excited. I remember, for the first time ever, experiencing being the one to sort out and take care of details for the two of us. It was an interesting role reversal being in charge of getting us around, having to admit that I got us lost, and having her look to me for the answers. I remember feeling honoured that she put that trust in me and that I could mother my mother for a short time.

Her visit to London was an opportunity to add her link to the generational chain I'd been following since I began reading your letters. It was another experience that would deepen our mother daughter bond. I remembered her telling me that she had travelled to England with you in her teens. I wondered what the dynamics of your relationship was like. Or what the dynamics between you and your mother Golda were.

Thinking back to changing dynamics reminds me of our trip to England as a family in 1995 to celebrate your 50th wedding anniversary with Papa. Seven of us came on that trip including you, Papa, Uncle Roger, Mom and Dad, and Ryan. Unlike this quickly planned trans-Atlantic trip, mom organized every detail of those 10 days we spent in your homeland. It was bittersweet because you were ill at the time. You were recovering from a stroke and much like the current trip opportunity was the driving force. It was another chance to see England with you, one that never came again because you past away three years later.

Over a glass of wine in a restaurant at the bottom of your street, we talked about the fact that in a way, this is the end of a chapter for me. Going forward, I will have a lovely, wonderful, and handsome husband, we will buy our first home, and we will be thinking of starting a family of our own. My life, as I know it, will be forever changed. Of course Mom and I can always promise to plan weekend mother daughter trips, but the truth is, two weeks together just her and I may not happen again. Life goes on, life changes as you make the beautiful decision to share your life with someone.

I assume you are nodding your head with a smile as you hear me say this, as you know exactly what I'm talking about. You made this kind of decision when committing to sharing your life with Papa. You turned the last page of the chapter in your life that you lived with your mum. Along with that decision was the reality that going the distance to Canada for the man you loved meant saying goodbye to your mum. That must have been hard, knowing that due to time, money and distance, there was a chance you may not see her again. I'm happy to know that you did see your mum once more, when you came over for Pauline's wedding in 1955. After that sail back to Canada across the Atlantic, it was then that you came home to tell Papa you were ready to have another baby: my mom.

Reading your letters gives me a glimpse into these incredible chapters of your life. Each and every one teaches me something, 67 years later. I can't help but think about those who will someday read the chapters of my life's letter and what they will learn from me.

With a granddaughter's love & admiration,
Carly
xox

CHAPTER 15

DEAR JANE & DEAR JOHN

A t this point, I had established a routine. I tried making it to my grandmother's neighbourhood at least once a week, but on occasion, I would go more than once if I needed to reconnect to her and my purpose. I'm not sure if it was the proximity to her front door that made me feel that connection or if it was the comfort food that the Italian café served, but something about the hours spent there fueled my soul. The waitress at Gastronomia La Delizia spoke little English, but knew my order at this point by heart: the Trieste Ciabattina, spicy smoked salmon with butter instead of mayo, coffee with steamed milk to start.

I had my colourful Post-Its ready, and I was diving into Grama's letters for the week ahead so that I could plan accordingly. It was my favourite thing about Mondays, because it always felt like I was sitting down for tea with her, just the two of us. My mom had just left, so I ordered a chocolate cookie for dessert to raise my spirits. I missed her already and it had only been a few hours.

My eyes read over a line in the letter dated March 27 1946 that made me stop in my tracks. It's as if all of the sounds around me suddenly come to a halt.

March 27, 1946

My Darling,
Here I am once again to fill one of these things up to try and tell you in words how much I love and miss you but I can never tell you in words darling how much I miss you. No letter again from

you today so I sure hope there are some in the morning for me. I hope you are okay darling and not working too hard. I am quite okay except for a slight cold but if I were with you darling I am sure there would be nothing wrong with me. Everything back here is very much the same. I have just come in from the Odeon, I saw 'The Spiral Staircase' it was quite good but I'm sure fed up with going to the pictures without you. Naty was here when I came in, Julia doesn't go out much as she is expecting her baby in May. It was another lovely day today so it looks as if spring has come to stay. I've had the window open in our room all day, it's still open now and I think I'll leave it open all night, I'm sure the air won't do me any harm. I have invited one of the girls from Farnborough to come here for the day on Saturday, so I suppose we'll have a real good jaw then. She married her Canadian January 25 and he sailed February 15 so I guess they have less married life than us, she's a nice kid and it will make a change to have someone here. I'll ask her to get those photos you asked for when she comes. The man about my camera came in the shop today and told me my camera was ready but when I went in there he discovered we had the wrong film in there as it takes a 620 not a 120 but now he said he'll have to get me another spool but he said he hopes to have it by Friday. Well darling, I guess that just about folds up the news for today, another lonely day without you (and not even a letter) but it's also another day behind us darling and another day nearer. I've never wished for time to go quick as much as I do now and it never has seem to go so slow and just think darling this time last year I hardly knew you and you were getting ready to tell me you were engaged to a girl in Canada remember? If I remember rightly this time last year I was going out with a ginger haired sergeant, but now I am a one man woman and I wouldn't go back to the old days for all the money in the world, in those days I was busy running away from wolves, now I'm running to one. The best and most wonderful husband in all the world. Good night darling. God bless you and pleasant dreams. Good luck. Au-revoir. All my love to you forever.

Your ever loving wifey,
Rene

I love you always in x's

Engaged? Wait, what?

Not only had she been in a relationship with a redheaded Air Force sergeant when they met, but my grandfather had been engaged. He must have popped the question right before he had left for the war and then met my grandmother.

My heart sank. Sometime between the time he and my grandmother got engaged and were married, my grandfather must have let his former fiancé know. Which meant he had told her one of two ways. He either sent a telegram or a letter . . . a Dear Jane letter.

My mind started to spiral. I wondered if Grama ever met her? Leamington is a small town, after all, and was even smaller then. Knowing Grama, I couldn't really see it fazing her much. The same way that she joked about her ginger sergeant, I couldn't really see her being the jealous type. My grandmother was so confident and sure of herself that she was like, "Meh, you were engaged before, but you're mine now!"

I wondered if my mom knew about this. Or if I should be going public with my family's story. Was I going to find out more family secrets that I had no business knowing about? Was I invading their privacy? Was this jilted fiancé still alive? It made me think back to my own dating history and the ways I got out of three serious long-term relationships. I was the one to walk away and I shamefully broke up with all three of them over email, a modern version of a Dear John letter. I was too wrapped up in my own stuff to do it any other way. I didn't have the strength and I was a coward. And I didn't have an ocean or a world war going on.

After I absorbed the shock of learning I shared my grandparents' Dear John/Dear Jane DNA, I began to feel more connected to them. For the first time since finding the letters, I started seeing them as more than just my grandparents – they were complex human beings. They were two people who had experienced love, heartbreak, loss, and forgiveness. I wondered what it was like for him to send that letter. Maybe decisions like this were easier during the war because they didn't want to waste time. They saw evidence of how fragile life was every single day and perhaps they followed their dreams, heart, and love more easily during that time. Life was too precious and fleeting to not follow love. They didn't have time to waste. We all have to make tough decisions in life. Decisions that might hurt someone and seem unfair in the moment, but that might ultimately spare people we care about from a lifetime of heartbreak.

I remember something shifting in that moment, and I felt like I was seeing my grandparents as people or peers for the very first time, fellow humans on the journey of life. I remember feeling a bit of relief. It's not just me. It's not just Adam. We both had serious relationships before. My grandparents had previous relationships, too. We are all complex individuals with experiences that shape us into who we are and that is okay. I felt so much guilt for breaking up with my previous boyfriends in the past in the way that I did, but this is life. If we open ourselves up to love, there is a possibility that someone may get hurt.

I wouldn't have wanted my grandparents to be with anyone else. They were blissfully happy together. I wouldn't have wanted Papa to stay with his previous fiancé out of a sense of duty or obligation. Following your heart is the most important thing.

Just as I had experienced the shift in the dynamics with my own mother, I was realizing that, as I was entering into adulthood and married life, I was starting to see my parents and my grandparents differently, too. They were not only caretakers for me as their child and grandchild anymore. They were fellow men and women with intricate life stories that made them who they are. I was connecting my own aches and joys with them, and feeling connected in all of our shared experiences through life.

The letters were a window into getting to know my grandmother as the woman she was. A woman like myself. I was just about the same age as her when she penned these letters. Of course they are the grandparents I remember, but these were the young grandparents I was just getting to know. A version of them that my own mother, their daughter, didn't know.

My mind flashed back to my ex-boyfriends. Up until this point, I had been so hard on myself for hurting them. Rightfully so. I had other options, but at the time, it seemed the only way. I was young and trying my best to follow my heart, even when it hurt. I realized that I still hadn't completely forgiven myself for the way I had ended things with each of them. In that moment, just as I was seeing my grandparents as humans, doing what needed to be done in the name of love, I was starting to see myself as a human, too. When I thought of the kind of love Grama and Papa shared though, I started to see that everything I had been through had made way for the love that I felt with Adam. I finally started to accept it had all worked out for the best for everyone, including my ex-boyfriends. In a way, this discovery felt refreshing. It made me feel like I could relate to my grandparents and see that even their epic love story that I had put on a pedestal for so long had its flaws. These things happen. We are human. This is love.

CHAPTER 16

PARK BENCHES

Throughout my days in London, I saw tiny reminders of how in sync my grandmother and I had become. It was a bit ironic because, growing up, she and I weren't overly close. I loved and adored her, but until this trip, I didn't understand her. Don't get me wrong, as a kid I couldn't wait to go to her house. She served tea and called me "love". But when we were out I would cringe because she was loud and the bull-in-a-china-shop-type. For birthdays, she would give me gifts that were always two years behind. I still remember the Sailor Moon watch she bought me because I had watched it a year or so before she gave it to me. By then, I had already moved on to boy bands and "Saved by the Bell". I was, however, in awe of her confidence. She dressed to impress and embraced her curves and most of the time she pulled it off. From time to time, she'd be the type to have lipstick smears on her teeth, but I loved seeing what sort of new fashion jewelry she'd be wearing upon each visit. It never dawned on me until we found the letters that many of the things I thought of as odd or eccentric about her was her Britishness. I knew she had an accent from England, but it never truly dawned on me she had emigrated to Canada from another country. It never occurred to me that some of her bravado might have been her way of masking the loneliness and homesickness that came from living so far away from her friends and family. At least not until I read Grama's letter from early April.

The letter came at the perfect time. I had been missing Adam and my family. I knew they would all be gathered around my parents' table for Easter dinner, and even though I was heading to Birmingham with Jess and Ollie to spend the holiday with Elyse and

Alec, I felt like I was missing out. There was always Facetime, but peering at faces all crammed together so I could see them on my laptop screen wasn't the same as being there. I still had months to go, and I was having a hard time showing up for the rest of the journey.

I was so self-absorbed that even when Jess needed me, I couldn't rally and be there for her. I had one of my biggest melt-downs since coming to England. At the time of my meltdown, she had just heard the news that her grandmother, back home in Leamington, had passed away. She had been 97 and had lived, by all accounts, an amazing, full life. I had planned a day out at St. James's Park to keep Jess' mind off of her loss and to do cre-ative fun things like painting and drawing once we got back to their flat. When her grandmother came up, we talked through her memories in a fun, playful way. We sat at her dining room table surrounded by paint and markers talking, reminiscing, and sitting comfortably with the silence in between. Jess was in the middle of telling me about her grandmother and what a wonderful person she had been, and I lost it. Jess of all people knew that sometimes we cannot help our emotions, and this was one of those times for me. There was no stopping it. I went into the bathroom, and my eyes filled with tears. She came in to check on me, and I fell into her arms and sobbed. I didn't want to go back to my flat. I didn't want to keep finding things to do until I left in June. I didn't want to admit to anyone how lonely I was. I didn't want to face my over-whelming guilt. I was in London, on a fabulous journey, and I was miserable. I couldn't believe I was being so incredibly selfish. The ever-present Positive Patty voice that rings in my head made me feel worse than I already did. Listen to yourself, Carly. You have SO much to be grateful for! So what, you are alone!? You are in London, England for goodness sakes! You should make EVERY day amazing because this is ONCE in a lifetime! Get yourself together! What kind of friend are you? You should be strong for Jess right now. If you have to feel this way can't you wait till later?

Of course, Jess being the incredible friend that she is spent the next hour reassuring me. Telling me she understood what I was going through. Assuring me that helping me was the best thing to help her get through her loss and it was better for her if I was real. I was so grateful for her in that moment.

One of the big lessons I was learning from my grandmother's letters and from my experience was the power of friends. I had always surrounded myself with friends growing up. In elementary and high school, it was quite common for me to have at least three or four friends over at a time, and I was always bringing people together.

I had been missing the connection that comes with sharing exactly what I was going through and the reassurance that comes from being authentic and real with people who knew me and loved me. As my grandmother was so fond of saying in her letters, having a "real jaw" with a friend helped any situation.

A few days after my big meltdown with Jess, I opened an email newsletter from Seth Godin:

The loneliness epidemic

The next time you feel lonely, disconnected or unappreciated, consider that unlike many other maladies, this one hits everyone. And unlike other challenges, this one is easily overcome by realizing that you can cure the problem by connecting, appreciating and leading.

The minute we realize that the person sitting next to us needs us (and our tribe, our forward motion and the value we create), we're able to extinguish their aloneness as well as ours.

When you shine a light, both of you can see better.

I hadn't realized until reading that email how lonely I had been. And I knew that the only remedy was to get out of my head and my flat and go out and meet people. The weather had been beautiful for a few days in a row, and I decided to check out new areas of London and just see where I would end up.

April 8, 1946

My Darling Husband,
Many thanks sweetheart for the two lovely letters that were wait-ing for me when I got in tonight. I hope this letter finds you in the best of health darling as this leaves me just dying for you. I have just come in from being out with two other brides, we had quite a pleasant evening, let our hair down and had a good jaw. We all seemed to be in better spirits tonight and full of rumours. Vera, has heard from somewhere that she should be going about the middle of May. She is about the same number as me so that's not bad is it darling? Doris has also heard that the Île de France is still taking brides without children so that also sounds good. That's all I'm living on these days darling, your letters and rumours but one of these days darling, P.G.E., I shall really get my sailing papers then we will be all set for perfect happiness. We went to the Lyons Corner House (you love that place don't you darling...anyway, it was somewhere to go and talk). We had supper then we went for ever such a long walk, right through St. James Park, we went past Buckingham Palace and had a good look at it as we kidded our-selves it would be the last time we would see it. Doris is the girl who is going to Welland, she says its 14 miles from the border, I thought you were on the border, darling. By the way darling, I weighed myself tonight and I weigh 9 stone, so I guess I have lost weight. (You will soon be able to lift me). But I guess I had better lose a bit more so as you can carry me over the threshold of our home, please God. Keep wishing and dreaming me over darling, because with both you and me wishing and dreaming, we might

get somewhere. I've got now that I don't care what they send me over in, a luxury liner or a cattle boat, anything as long as it takes me into your arms, darling. A bride to-night said she hasn't written to her husband for over a week and she was only married in December. I don't know how she can be in love with him and not write, I feel much better after I have written to you, I feel just as if I had had a good talk with you, but it's a very, very poor substitute to talking to you darling, as well you know sweetheart. I guess that rounds off the news for another lonely day today without my darling husband but all we can do is hope and pray that it won't be long now. The clothing coupons started today so I think I will treat myself to something this week. Now I guess I'll toddle off to bed, darling to get some more beauty sleep. Good-night my dearest darling, God Bless You and may all your dreams be pleasant. Good Luck. Au-revoir.
Your everloving wifey,
Rene

I LOVE YOU (in x's) N.H.Wiebe

April 9, 2013

Dear Grama,
I was so excited to read that you spent some time in Central London. I'll take any excuse to spend a day wandering a place that thousands of tourists from around the world come to every day. It's especially easy now that the weather is getting nicer and we're actually having quite a few sunny days. Being in London sure does make me appreciate them when they come around.

This specific day I spent at a café in St. James's Park, called "Inn the Park." As I was sitting having a wonderful lunch on the patio while I journalled, wrote out some postcards, and read, I started to get curious about the "Lyons Corner House" that you spoke of. After doing a handy Google search, I realized that the place that you and Papa loved so much was no longer there. It had been open from around 1909 to 1977. I thought it would be great to find where it was when it existed and I at least knew it was on "the Strand."

As I ventured up and down the famous street, I had high hopes that there'd be an old sign that one would imagine they'd typically find on English buildings saying something like, Here stood the old Lyons Corner House. Sounds like something that would be in a historically rich country. Too much to ask? After a nice long walk looking buildings up and down as if I were sizing them up, I decided that I'd better ask someone or else I'd be doing this all day. Going into a hotel to ask a concierge felt like a great idea. As I walked into a rather swanky hotel on the Strand, I brought out your letter and asked the man if he knew where the old "Lyons Corner House" used to be. The middle-aged man's eyes lit up as if I had brought back a sweet memory for him. He went on to say that it was where the bookstore now stood, on the corner facing Trafalgar Square. I asked him if he had ever been there and what he remembered about it. "Why yes," he went on to say, "my mum used to take me there as a young boy. I remember having tea and great meals there. It was a lovely place." As he finished, a curious look came over his face, probably due to the fact that a young gal with a North American accent would ask such a thing. I told him my story, he said it was a pleasure to share his memories and wished me well on my journey.

My next stop was the bookstore, where I browsed the shelves, wandered the aisles and made my way up to the coffee shop on the second floor. I ordered myself a tea and found a free seat next to the window. I looked out at the spectacular view of the Admiralty Arch between Trafalgar Square and the Mall that leads to Buckingham Palace. I took a few moments to imagine what it was like in the 40s. Whenever I do that, my mind always seems to change the colours of today, into black & white. As I took a quick snap with my phone, changed the settings to black & white, and really took it all in, I thought about the fact that I was, yet again, sharing a view with you.

As I continued my walk through St. James Park up towards Buckingham Palace, I turned back to have one last glance of the mighty building that, I imagine, represented so much for you: Familiarity. Nostalgia. Loyalty. Home.

With a granddaughter's love & admiration,
Carly
xoxox

To battle the loneliness, I started making a habit of taking long walks and sitting down next to someone on a park bench and striking up a conversation. It wasn't long until I found myself in deep, meaningful, soul connections with complete strangers, which reminded me of my days behind the wicket. My favourite chance meeting was the day that I spent wandering through Regent's Park and stumbled upon Queen Mary's Garden. It seemed fitting with my strong connection to all things Queen Mary, and the waterfalls and spring flowers in bloom were simply stunning. As I sat on a bench for a snack, the most interesting woman sat down beside me. It wasn't long until we started chatting.

Her name was Brownie Dene, a 93-year-old beauty, still wearing lipstick that was a little smudged, big sunglasses with tape on the middle, and high heel wedges, sitting and soaking up the sun. The second she started talking, she reminded me of my grandmother. Accent, lipstick, heels, and all. Brownie had been a theatre star in the 30s and told me all about her life, her husband, and how she came up with her stage name. She told me that theatre was the love of her life and that her theatre family was the only family she had left. She told me about how she wrote stories over a cuppa all of her life and enjoyed the creativity of writing immensely.

"You don't sound British, where are you from?" she asked.

"My grandmother was British, and I'm here retracing the steps of her 110 love letters that I found from 1946," I explained.

"Oh my goodness, I've heard about you, I heard you on the radio!" She then explained that she was partially blind and her friends had told her about seeing me on BBC Breakfast. "I can't wait to tell my friends that I met that Canadian gal that's here retracing her grandmother's steps."

I couldn't believe that she had actually heard of me. Imagine!

We talked about her experience during the war and how she was 19 and went to Africa as a military performer for 18 months. Our interaction was just amazing, and after about 30 minutes, I asked her if we could get a picture together. She gave me her address to keep in touch, and I knew that I wanted to see her again or at least become penpals.

Just as she was leaving, she leaned over and gave me a hug. "From your grandma," she said as she touched my face. "I can see your beautiful face." With that, she was gone, and I watched her walk on with her sight cane. She paused for a moment at the waterfall and took the sound and what sight she could see in before turning the corner to catch her taxi.

It left me stunned and filled with gratitude. I actually did feel like it was a hug from my grandmother. Meeting Brownie Dene taught me so much. Here was a woman who was nearly blind and quite old, yet she didn't talk about loneliness or regret. She still looked forward each day to getting dressed, doing her hair, putting on her lipstick, and getting out in the world. Even if it was just to sit in the park and chat with a young girl looking for someone to talk to. I had tears in my eyes and said a little prayer of gratitude to my grandmother, thanking her for passing down her chatterbox gene because the people I kept meeting on this journey within her journey were beyond special.

April 25t, 1946

My Darling Nick,
Since seeing that little bit in the paper to-night that I am enclos-ing to you I have been so excited you would think I had my sailing papers already. You must agree with me darling that although it's not my sailing papers yet it's certainly good news, anyway ever since reading it I have felt all funny inside and I feel I must just sit down and write to you. Many thanks darling for the letter I got from you this morning, I hope you are okay darling as this leaves me but loving you and missing you as much as ever of course, more than ever if that's possible. Doris also rang me up to tell me about the Queen Mary to-night as soon as she read it she said she had also heard that they have reached 32,000, so that's only another 8000 to go before they reach my number, anyway Doris' number is 38,000, so as soon as I hear she is going I won't have long to wait, P.G. Nothing else much happened to-day, I have just come in from work and as Dixie is asleep I let Janey go to the pic-tures so I am alone here, Mum is in bed again because she doesn't feel well again and the doctor is supposed to come to-night to see her. Darling please don't think that anything you write will ever bore me because it never will, just like the song, every letter that you send me I read a dozen times or more, just because you write it darling, sometimes when I start a letter I usually think whatever am I going to find to write about but some how or oth-er the words usually come pouring out, I guess it's because I'm a natural born chatter box, but I guess you know that by now. I went in about my snaps to-day but they were still not ready so I guess you'll still have to wait darling to see how I look now but I think I still look the same as when you left me maybe a little thinner, but I don't think you will find anything missing, gee! This thinking

below the belt must be catching aren't you ashamed of your wifey darling? Still you always did say I would turn into a wolfess didn't you sweet? Well I guess I'll have to close now darling as I'm near the end. Good-night darling. God Bless You and pleasant dreams. Good-Luck. Au-revoir. Hope to see you soon. All my love to you forever.
Your ever loving wifey,
Rene

I LOVE YOU (in x's)

Brownie in the park

April 25, 2013

Dear Grama,

Oh, your excitement has got me all excited, too! With every letter, I feel as if I'm reading a book that I already know the ending to, yet it's still so engaging. Your giddiness about the Queen Mary is an accurate one, and as you've mentioned in a few letters from last week as well, you seem to have a funny feeling about it and even dreaming about it. I'll go ahead and say that even 67 years ago, intuition, gut feelings and believing that fate will so graciously work it's magic...was alive and well. I love those kinds of feelings.

Following your lead, I'm going to go ahead and say that I have a good feeling about my journey on the Queen Mary II. Yes you heard correctly, Grams. I'm setting sail a day after your sailing date on the RMS Queen Mary II. Oh...I know, I know...I'm gushing, too. I have a funny feeling that I'm bound to meet some pretty phenomenal people on the lone voyage across the Atlantic. I arrive at the New York City port and plan to make my way home via train, just as you did.

It's been a stunningly gorgeous week and I have officially lost track of the days of sunshine. I'm not sure if it's that, or the countdown I have going, but I am continually having days when I just wish I could bottle up the gratitude. This country is amazing and in springtime it's even more fabulous. British park culture is in full swing and I am loving it.

When I had my interview on Tuesday at the BBC for CBC, I spent the afternoon in a small park near some offices not far from Oxford Circus. It was so amazing seeing all of the business professionals coming out for lunch break picnics, taking in the sun. Yesterday I was in a more residential park and made friends with a few new moms and their little ones.

Today's meeting was perhaps the best of all...a 93-year-old woman who told me all about her thriving theatre career that began in the 30s. After a wonderful visit, she said it was so nice to be honoured to meet the Canadian gal who's been all over the news. She had remembered me from my media frenzy back in February. So, needless to say...thank you for the chatter box gene because the people I'm meeting on this journey within your journey, are beyond incredible.

With a granddaughter's love & admiration,

Carly
xoxox
ps...you're so cheeky...you wolfess, you.

CHAPTER 17

CHOICES

The crown jewel in my search for connection had to be Harry, who goes by the epic name of Legend. I met him on May 1 on the day that my grandmother went to the Hippodrome to watch a play. I set out in search of the Hippodrome, but was disappointed to find it shuttered and closed. The sign was still there, but the building was vacant. I settled for plan B that day and counted my blessings that this was a first. Up until this point, I had found almost everything I went out searching for. If Grama saw a play, then I could at least change course and head to the theatre district instead. It was early afternoon and the shows didn't start until the evening, so I stopped to sit in St. James's Park, taking a seat next to an older man.

"Nice day, isn't it?" was my go to line. Harry was quick to join the conversation. He told me that he had worked in security for a long time and had met the Queen and a number of movie stars. He was a security guard for Elizabeth Taylor for a little while and had accidently stepped on her son's foot at his wedding, which he explained wouldn't have been a big deal except they were hippies and got married barefoot.

We chatted about theatre and how he still enjoyed working at one well into his 70s. When I marveled at him working so long, he told me that people comment on that all the time. And he always tells them the same thing, "We are all given a choice. We can sit around in our room and be lonely or we can get out and be Legend."

"I choose Legend," he said.

After he bid his farewell, I sat thinking about what he had said. Meeting Harry had been a sign. Before he had a chance to get too far away, I ran after him and asked him if he had any tips for getting last-minute tickets for his theatre. He told me to come with him. He showed me the queue for returned tickets and after about 40 minutes, I got the last one available for 20 pounds. A 60-pound saving over the regular 80-pound price. Thank you, Harry.

May 1, 1946

My Darling,
Many thanks sweetheart for the letter I got this afternoon. I hope you are fine darling as this leaves me but missing you like hell. Nothing very much exciting happened to-day, this afternoon as it was my half-day I did Janey's shopping up at John Barnes and then I rang up both Doris and Vera and we had a little chat. Doris told me that the Île de France is sailing on Wednesday with brides so that made us very happy, even if we are not going on it, its all those nearer to us anyway. It would really be lovely if I would go with either Doris or Vera but I don't really care darling because I know at the end of the voyage you will be waiting for me and that thought would keep me going if everything else went wrong darling, but I have a funny idea everything is going to be lovely, I only hope it's soon, please God. I have just come in from the Golders Green Hippodrome. I thought it would make a change, it was quite good, I saw Henry Hall and his Orchestra, he's got a smashing band and I could hardly stop myself from getting up and dancing to it. Remember when we nearly went there darling to see pantomime but when we got there it didn't start until Sat so we went all over London and finished up at the Met, Edgeware Rd., remember? I suppose building a house would be a very good idea darling, but I guess you're right and it's better to wait until we get to-gether and then we can really talk it over. I guess you just about know me by now because I am going to say that anything you do will be alright because you are the best and cleverest husband in all the wide world and I know you think things over a lot before you decide. That girl yesterday really made me mad

(the one who got her sailing papers) because she didn't seem at all
pleased and she said "I'm sorry I started it all now, aren't you?"
and I said "Of course not, I'll do it all over again." And I would
darling, because I love you and only you for the rest of my life.
Well sweetheart I guess that's the news for another day, it was
a lovely day for the 1st of May and let's hope May will be a lucky
month for us. A guy spoke to me while I was waiting for the bus
this morning, he said, "you look happy," so I said, "well it's the
1st May and a lovely day, so why not?" Well now I guess I'll have
to sign off so good-night my darling. Please look after yourself
for me. God Bless You and pleasant dreams, darling. Good-luck.
Au-revoir. Hope to see you soon. All my love to you forever.
Your everloving wifey,
Rene

I LOVE YOU (in x's)

May 1, 2013

Dear Grama,
Oh I had the most incredible day today, I could just scream
from the rooftops just how amazing life is and how magical
it is to be here retracing your steps. I had a wonderful lunch
with Genevieve, someone I now consider to be a very close
friend. I met her while finding my wedding dress, actually. She suggested we meet at Liberty, which I'm sure you
loved back in your day. We browsed some shops & had a
lovely lunch. Dessert, the infamous carrot cake, was to die
for. After our 4 hour lunch date and amazing conversation,
I made my way to St. James's Park to soak up the sun. As
I sat on the park bench, I couldn't help but feel curious
about the man sitting next to me. I'm not sure if this has
happened since living on my own over here, but I just love
chance-meeting conversations. You never know what will

unfold or who you'll end up meeting and becoming friends with. This man was in his 70s and once our conversation began, I knew I was meant to meet him. He told me all about the time that he spent with Elizabeth Taylor, his one liner words of wisdom that he lives by, and all about why he still works, well into his 70s, at a place he adores: the theatre. The chance meeting couldn't have been more perfect, because this very day, 67 years earlier, you had been to see a performance at a theatre.

After we bid each other a lovely farewell, I felt like meeting him was a sign from you, so I decided to catch up with him and walk in the direction of the theatres. I asked him which theatre he worked at and if it was possible to get last minute tickets. He told me all the in's and out's and showed me where to queue up for returns. I ended up getting an £80 ticket for £27.50 and the show was phenomenal. It was Peter & Alice, which is about Alice in Wonderland & Peter Pan all grown up, starring Judi Dench and Ben Wishaw. The performance left me deeply moved and I, yet again, found myself in the middle of Central London fighting back the tears as I ran to catch the tube. The message of the performance was that life is a choice. We all grow up, bad things happen in life and it's all part of the journey. We can choose to dwell on it and let it take over our lives, or choose acceptance in life. It left me with a very obvious urgency to live my life to the fullest. It made me want to make the most of my every day. In the end that's all we've got: CHOICE. That message was illustrated so well in Judi Dench's line, "I could be the old woman who saw the last of her days lonely in a room somewhere...or I could be Alice. I choose Alice." A few hours earlier, on the park bench in St. James's Park, Legend (what the gentleman I met goes by...no joke) looked at me and said: "The reason I still work in my 70s is because of something I heard in a play once...I could be lonely sitting in a room somewhere...or I could be Legend...I choose Legend."

Grama, you sure did the same in life. You chose life. You chose happiness. You chose Rene. The bright, bold, bubbly, make the most of this life, Rene.

With a granddaughter's love & admiration,

Carly
Xoxo
Ps...I choose Carly

CHAPTER 18

A SPECIAL BOND

In one of the last letters, my grandmother spoke about going to see her brother Joe and his wife Phoebe, and she asked my grandfather to "drop them a few lines." She put their address at the bottom of the letter so I followed her lead and ventured to the address she penned to my grandfather six decades earlier. So much of London was destroyed. The heaviest bombing came during the blitz, whole neighbourhoods had to be rebuilt after the war. I wasn't sure what I would find. Walking through the neighbourhood Google had directed me to, it didn't look too promising as I passed numerous new developments. Turning a corner, I saw an older looking building. As I got closer, I could see the sign commemorating the building's age and historical importance. I was standing in front of the very building my grandmother had visited so many years prior.

I felt a deep bond between myself and my grandmother, between her past and my present, between her younger self and myself as the young woman she didn't live to know. Yes, I've been extremely *lucky* to see all of the places our shared journey allowed me to experience, all the buildings and sites, homes and shops still standing that have connected me with her again and again. But it wasn't mere luck that brought me to each point along the way, it was my grandmother's pride in her city, the excitement she shared with my grandfather in her letters about even the smallest parts of her day, and the love she showed for the people and the places that sustained her as she waited to leave. I realized standing in front of the building that this may have been one of the last times she spent with her brother before she sailed away. I wondered how many times she would see them again? Did they write letters back and forth that were read and re-read and then eventually thrown away? And I thought about how hard it would be to only see my family on rare occasions. My family was such an intricate part of who I was. Yes, I had travelled the world and left for a year here and there, but to give up everything?

My brother and his wife Sulienne were scheduled to arrive later that week, and I couldn't wait to see them. I couldn't wait to be with family again. To show Ryan our Grama's London.

Growing up, Ryan and I looked like twins and were close in age. We were 17 months apart. Of course, we had our fights like all siblings do, but the roles of the older protective brother and the doting little sister were always strong. A few years prior, my parents brought out the VHS tapes of our first few Christmases as a family of four. I couldn't help but smile when I saw Ryan proudly showing off his new Velcro shoes to me, as I lovingly encouraged him and told him how "spiffy" they were. We loved each other and were quite close, all things considered.

Sulienne had been in our lives since a few months after my grandmother passed away. Grama would have loved her. Like our Grama, she was full of life and wonder. She had a passion for travel, adventure, and seeing the world. She absolutely loved London. This was her first visit. It was such a treat watching her immerse herself in the history of the city, the amazing stories of the British royal family, and pure magic that London has to offer.

She and Ryan started dating when I was 14, and she treated me more like an adored little sister than her boyfriend's bratty sibling. We had a bond. And whenever we were together we launched into deep, loving, honest, and inspiring conversations. I loved Ryan too, but he was mostly along for the ride. He was happy if he was making Sulienne happy. As long as he got to visit a few of the pubs that Shakespeare frequented and go to the dog races, Ryan would be happy.

I made arrangements for us to go to dog races near Wimbledon to commemorate the activities that Grama did with her siblings before she got her sailing papers. She had talked about going to the dogs several times with her brother Joe. And of course we took in the sights. We went on a bus tour, walked the Thames, stopping at old pubs along the way, and visited the Tower of London, as we had in 1995. On the morning of our Tower of London tour, I opened my email to a quick note from my mom and dad, with an attached photo of Ryan and I standing on guard in front of the black posting boxes. The serious expressions on our 10- and 11-year-old faces made us giggle. We walked through Grama's old neighbourhood and I showed them some of the places I'd visited that she had written about.

Sulienne went on a day tour to Bath, Stonehenge, and Salisbury by herself on one of their last days in England, while I went to pick up my wedding dress, and my brother enjoyed the British Netflix options that weren't available back home. She couldn't wait to see the Magna Carta, stand among the mystery of the famous stones, and buy some Roman bathwater. Dropping Sulienne off at the bus tour meet up point felt like I was dropping her off to her first day of school. It made me proud of both of us in that moment. She was on her own to go on an adventure for the day, something that I had somehow become accustomed to over the past few months. It was as if, in that moment, she were holding up a mirror for me to see all that I had accomplished being over here on my own. I saw bravery and courage in her that morning venturing off on her own, and that strength created a silent bond between the two of us that would be with us forever.

The night before they left, Ryan said something to me that will stay with me forever. He told me how happy he was for Adam and I. How thrilled he was that I'd found someone who could take care of me in a way that I willingly welcome a man to – fixing the car, hanging the blinds, carrying heavy things from the basement, and coming to my rescue when anything breaks. Things that Ryan, who had been just a phone call away during my two years of single living in my apartment in Windsor, had been there to do. As we were finishing up our last dinner together and clinking our glasses cheering the wonderful holiday we'd spent together, he nonchalantly mentioned that I could always call him, even if I didn't have anything for him to fix. And he told me he loved me.

The love that siblings share is special. It's powerful knowing that someone has your back. It's a bond that no matter where life takes you, you know that the strength of your relationship is enough to withstand the distance. A distance that is immeasurable, really. My guess is that it's the kind of love that could go the distance of the Atlantic...20 times over.

June 10, 1946

My Darling,
Once again I settle down darling to write you a few lines, which I sure hope I won't have to do soon now, P.G. This is the fourth day I haven't heard from you and I sure hope it's because of the holidays. I hope you are quite okay darling as this leaves me but longing and just anxiously waiting for when I can be with you again. It has still been a holiday here in England. Bank holiday Monday, I know you don't have that one in Canada. After waking up this morning and being disappointed because there were no letters, I mooched around, made a cake and done a few odd jobs. Then after lunch I met Doris in Piccadilly (remember the red light, darling?). First of all we took in a show, saw a film called "From this day forward." It was a lovely film all about a couple who had just got married so of course Doris and I enjoyed it but boy did we ever wish we had our husbands with us. I really do think though that Doris and I should hear any day now because it's two weeks ago now when Ethel got her papers. When we came out of the pictures we went and had supper, then we walked all down the Mall right to Buckingham Palace and saw all the decorations. We also saw the Royal Stand where the King and Queen stood and saluted everyone. It was quite interesting but I still wouldn't have cared if I hadn't seen it. In the last two letters I wrote darling, I put our

new address on it, I hope I have spelt it right but if I haven't don't blame me it's the way you wrote it, but I think I'll wait to address this one to make sure of the address from the letters I hope to get in the morning, please God. Janey just said 'it's a shame you aren't here because there are a lot of Cowboy films on now.' I don't have to tell you I sure wish you were here now, it would have been especially nice if you could have met Albert, I know you two would have got on smashing to-gether. Never mind darling, just let us two get to-gether again, P.G. then everything will be fine. Now I guess its time for me to hit the hay for another lonely night darling, but I sure hope those nights are numbered now darling. Good-night sweet. God Bless You and Sweet Dreams to you. Good Luck. Au-revoir. Hope to see you soon. All my love to you forever.
Your everyloving wifey,
Rene

I LOVE YOU (in x's)

Ryan, Carly, and Julienne at Wimbledon Stadium

June 20th, 2013

Dear Grama,

Sorry that it's been a while since I've written. I've been so busy in quite possibly the best way. I had Ryan & Sulienne here visiting for 10 whole days and this letter was the first day of their visit. Naturally I brought them to Central London despite their fading eyes after a night of travel. The lights and excitement of Piccadilly sure woke them up and they were both in awe as I led them through the city center with ease that even surprised me. I really have gotten to know your city, Grams. I even must have that air about me, because aimless tourists approach me on a regular basis asking for directions. I secretly love it.

I could sit and list all the things we experienced together, but that would be the longest letter imaginable, so I will sum up our time together as best as I can. We laughed like siblings do. We shared the teeny tiny space of my flat and came out of it with only a few bruises. We fought like siblings do. And most importantly, we cherished the moments we got to share together like most siblings forget to do.

Sulienne has been in our lives since a few months after you left us. Grama, you would love her. She is full of life and wonder, and has a passion for travel, adventure and seeing the world. She absolutely loved the history of your city, the amazing stories of the royal family, and pure magic that London has to offer. She truly has been like a sister to me since they started dating when I was 14. I am grateful for our bond and the loving, honest and inspiring conversations that were had.

Ryan was mostly along for the ride, getting excited about making Sulienne happy, enjoying visiting the pubs that

Shakespeare frequented, and going to the dog races. I imagine him & your brothers would have "got on smashingly" as well. He also really enjoyed seeing your neighbourhood and honouring this journey in his own special way. The night before they left, he said something to me that will stay with me forever. It was about how happy he was for Adam and I. Specifically how thrilled he was that I had found someone that can take care of me in a way that I personally need a man to. Fixing the car, hanging the blinds, carrying heavy things from the basement and coming to my rescue when anything breaks. Things that Ryan was just a phone call away to do during my two years of single-living in my apartment in Windsor. As we were finishing up our last dinner together and clinking our glasses in cheers of a great holiday, he nonchalantly mentioned that I am to always call him, even if I don't have anything for him to fix. He loves me.

Having them both here made me think a lot about how your siblings must have felt about you making the big move across the pond. I am sure they were beyond happy for you, and I am also sure there was a bit of sadness in seeing you go. Of course it's all a part of life and we all grow up and get on with our own lives and families and at the same time recognizing that the end of eras create a bit of nostalgia.

The love that siblings share is special. It's a beautiful thing. It's a bond that no matter where life brings you, its strength is enough to withstand the distance. Almost immeasurable, really. My guess is that it's the kind of love that could go the distance of the Atlantic...20 times over.

With a granddaughter's love & admiration,
Carly Xoxox

CHAPTER 19

ONLY LETTERS

I was officially one month away from the day my ship would set sail. Earlier on in the journey, Adam and I had discussed spending a period of time using letter writing as our main and only form of communication. Since the beginning, I could communicate with Adam and my family through text and Facebook, Skype and email. Rarely had a few hours gone by, much less a day, that I hadn't heard from someone back home. To really understand the separation my grandmother had endured, I wanted to spend the last month as she had, communicating with Adam and my parents only through letters. My parents were seeing Adam regularly and I knew I would be tempted to ask them how he was on a daily basis, so I did the same with them as well.

We did some calculations, and Day One of Only Letters coincided with the day of Ryan and Sulienne's departure. Saying goodbye to my visitors and halting instant communication with three of my biggest supports all in one day probably wasn't my brightest idea, but I knew it was something I wanted to do. Letter writing immediately felt different from that day on. My love for receiving letters quadrupled overnight, and I couldn't wait for the postman to come by our group of flats on his daily rounds.

It also just so happened to be an excruciating time for my grandmother in 1946, as well. As I read through her letters from some of these first few days of instant communication silence between Adam and I, she mentioned reading about a tornado in the papers that had torn through the Windsor, Ontario region killing 17 people, which was the exact region, my grandfather was now living in. It wasn't until four days later that she was able to breathe a sigh of relief to hear that he was safe and unharmed.

Letter writing is such a unique form of communicating. Since the beginning, so many people shared their experiences of letter writing with me. They shared what it was like to have to wait to hear from the one you love for sometimes up to two weeks or how the best part of the day was going to the post office or checking the mailbox. We now have instant communication like never before. Communicating through cursive and experiencing the unique longing and anticipation is truly only possible in this time if deliberately arranged.

The minute my self-imposed communication ban started, time seemed to slow down, and I began to notice how much of our time is spent in virtual connecting. Was it real? I knew it sure wasn't as good as in person connection. Part of me knew that just as my grandmother and grandfather used the most modern forms of technology that they had at the time – telegrams, letters, etc. – we were just working with what we had, but did gaining that level of virtual connection make us lose something along the way? I started to pay attention to the world around me and how we connect.

Removing the connection from Adam and my parents seemed to heighten my senses and emotions. Although I spent most of my days connected to the rest of the world through Facebook, Instagram, Twitter, email, texting, letters, and just about every other form of technology, loneliness reared its head again. It didn't matter how many virtual connections I had received that day, what I longed for the most was physical touch, someone's presence, or a conversation – live in real time.

It wasn't until a moment in Starbucks near Southbank when it all started to sink in for me. All I could have ever wished for was someone to sit across from me and share a story or engage in meaningful conversation, when I noticed two girls sitting beside me. Mid-conversation, one of them took out her phone and took a selfie with her mocha frocca latte frappuccino – cutting her friend off completely, to show her Instagram and Facebook friends what she was up to. It rocked me. It didn't make sense. We had things so backwards it hurt my soul, my heart, and my ego when I actually thought about the amount of times I had done it, too.

Of course, I saw the perks of it all. We can keep in touch in this now very small world because of it all. Technology allowed me to share my journey with so many people around the world. I could get a daily dose of cuteness from a Japanese hedgehog I followed on Instagram. But something was happening, and I felt like I was seeing it with fresh eyes for the first time. It made me think of how the different generations experience these forms of communication. I'm sure the generations before mine were all amazing and a little confused by it all; my generation was thankfully free of it during our high school years and saw it evolve into our adulthood, but every generation after mine would just grow up with it and not know any different.

It was becoming clear to me during those days that the most profound aspects of my journey were the people I met. On a park bench, in a library, or at a café, I noticed the connection between people and what good, old-fashioned connection had to go up against in this time: cell phone notifications, cameras, texts, selfie photo ops. I couldn't help but wonder if we were losing the ability to truly connect with one another anymore.

I desperately wanted to remember this feeling, this desire to put my phone away and connect with the world around me. I wanted to remember this when I was reunited with all of those I love the most.

CHAPTER 20

GRAMA'S LAST LETTER

D espite the extra reasons for missing Adam, the days started to fly by. I was taking a lot of pictures, getting outside and exploring every day. I met up with friends, old and new, and I was really starting to feel at home in London. I wasn't simply doing what Grama did, I was using her journey to create my own. I went to all the places she went and did the things she did, but I began accompanying her activities with mine.

I officially became a regular at the Italian café around the corner from Grama's house. They knew me as the girl writing a book. I went there at least three times a week. Occasionally, I went to the historical wine bar called the Arches at the end of her street. After hearing my story, the owners told me that it was a bakery in the 40s. They showed me the old brick wood fire oven in the basement, and the character of that place alone told its history. I wondered if it was where Grama got her bread.

I rotated between writing in cafés and other inspiring and beautiful places. I loved going to the British Library, which is the largest library in the world. The main reading room is massive and lined with beautiful vintage books. It always felt like an inspiring place to be. The Westminster Library was a favourite, housed in a gray stone building that made me think of Jane Austen every time. It had free WiFi and was close to the Leicester Square tube stop. After settling in, I would write letters to Adam, write a blog post, or get lost in a book, always surprised at how quickly the time flew.

I read *Pictures at an Exhibition* there after I heard from Camilla MacPherson, the author who contacted me through my blog. She had heard one of the interviews I'd done about my project. Her novel was eerily similar to my story, both with aspects of letters and the historical versus current day perspective. The differences were that hers was fictional and had the added element of paintings at the National Gallery. We met up for tea a few times and discussed writing and stories and our lives. She was in her mid-30s, had blonde hair, kind eyes, and on the first day we met, we coincidentally both wore red coats. She had an adorable young daughter who I got to meet on a few occasions. She told me about the year she took off from her law practice to pursue her writing. She giggled and warned me about the entire day she spent researching what stamps looked like in the 40s that wound up being a few descriptive words on one page. An entire day for a few words! It reminded me of my flop of a day at the British National Archives in Kew Gardens, only to find that every document that had anything to do with my grandmother unfortunately wouldn't load. She explained how rewarding it was to finally have a published book and told me how she handled reading reviews. She gave me some tips on WWII research in London and told me places to avoid. Our interactions were always sweet, and I felt like I was getting advice from a wise older sister, from someone who had gone down the path. There was also the sense that she could really only tell me so much, that I would have to go down the path of writing my first book to really discover some of the things one goes through in the process. It felt nice to be seen, though, and to have someone encourage me and wish me luck with a knowing smile. We even met up at the Charles Dickens museum before I left. We thought it was fitting.

After experiencing bouts of loneliness throughout this trip, I'd made a point of making plans with people I knew every week. I went out for dinner with Harry one night after seeing a play starring Daniel Radcliffe. We went for mussels, fries, and wine at a great French restaurant, and he entertained me with more theatre stories. I never got tired of Harry's inside scoop on what went on behind the velvet curtain.

In between all of my plans and busyness, I began to realize that the letters that had guided me for the first two-thirds of my trip were about to come to an end. The letters that brought me on this quest and sparked the simple but slightly crazy idea of living in London for six months just as my grandmother had 67 years earlier strangely ended one month before her departure. There must have been more letters over those last few weeks, more I miss yous, more of her funny comings and goings sent to her love across the ocean, but they were not among the bundle my mom found when she packed up my grandfather's home.

I wished sitting there in the library, thinking about the final month that lay ahead, that I could talk to my grandmother. I wanted to ask her, "Am I doing this right, Grama? Is this what you wanted when you guided me to find the letters to take up this crazy trip? There have been too many signs that have told me that you are guiding all of this. Are you okay with it? Making your letters public on this BIG OLD interweb craziness, that I'm sure you would find amazing and nonsensical, all at the same time. I know you would be especially smitten with all the media attention you, and because of you, I have received. Growing up, I remember seeing British newspapers sprawled among the Leamington Post and Windsor Star in your living room, *The Daily Mirror* always at the top of the pile. We made it into *The Daily Mirror*, Grama. Are you proud?"

Thinking about the gap between the end of the letters and my sailing date 24 days away on the RMS Queen Mary II, I wondered if I had gotten the point of the trip. What impact will this have? Will anyone besides me care once it is over? I was hoping to inspire people in some way. To give people the courage to show up in their own lives. To go after a dream or an inspiration, even if it didn't make sense to anyone else. To follow an idea as far as they could, especially when it was inspired by someone they loved and admired. I wanted to encourage people to express themselves creatively, however that looked to them: through the lyrics of a song, through the hands crafting a quilt, through the colours on a canvas, through the lens of a camera, through a poem, or through a lovingly home-cooked meal. Most of all, I wanted to encourage others to write their own *Life's Letter*.

I realized that was exactly what I had been doing since the day in Long Beach, California when inspiration struck out of nowhere after recreating the photo at the Queen Mary. It was exactly what I had been doing with every letter retraced and with every step I took on this journey in England. But now it was up to me to define my time. Grama had been my guide for the first part of the journey — I would be my guide for the last.

BY AIR MAIL

AIR LETTER

IF ANYTHING IS ENCLOSED
THIS LETTER WILL BE SENT
BY ORDINARY MAIL.

POSTAGE 6 6

Mr. Nick Wiebe
61, Clark St. W.
Leamington
Ontario
Canada

Second fold here →

To open cut here →

Sender's name and address :-

Mrs. W. H. Wiebe
21 Steigher Place
W. Hampstead London N.W.6
England

← To open cut here

143

14/6/46

My Darling Nick,

Many thanks sweetheart for the two letters I got this afternoon. I hope this finds you okay darling as it leaves me but very very lonely for a certain handsome guy who by the way happens to be my husband (the best in all the whole wide world) I have a bit of good news for you to-night darling. Doris got her papers this morning and very short notice she has to be ready at 24 hrs notice from to-morrow, I reckon the papers have been held up because of the holidays. Her number is 38,616, so soon, please God you can look out for your little wifey, after them telling me at the repat office yesterday they had reached 38,600, I knew Doris would leave very soon. Now I know its nead the waiting seems worse than ever, I can't sleep at all these nights, last night I thought I would go crazy, tossing and turning there, I

144

think

2

its all the excitement. I am glad
you are getting on with the sink
darling and that you have made
it special low for me. I think you
are a real angel for trying to get
everything done, but please don't
worry yourself too much darling about
everything, I am sure everything will
work out lovely, esp. if we are
to-gether to figure it all out, with
you beside me darling I shan't
care about a damn thing. The only
thing I worry about is that I hope
I get used to everything quickly
because I know a lot of things
are different over there, to here,
one thing I know I mustn't ask for
a joint in the butcher. I don't
mind a bit about your teeth darling,
you'll always be good-looking and
I shall love you in fifty years
time just as much as I do, by
the way darling I didn't marry
you for your looks, but you sure are
handsome. Casanova, I'm sorry I

145

couldn't resist that. By the way
darling is our house nearer to
the factory then yours mothers
was? I can just see you now
some of these mornings, P. G soon
jumping out of bed and dashing
round so as you won't be late in
the morning, I guess that will be
one of my wifely jobs eh! Well
sweetheart I guess thats the
news for another night such as it
is, but it won't be long now
darling, whoopee, when I can stop
writing to you I shall be the
happiest girl in the world, but I
thank God that we started writing
nearly two years ago darling. Now
I suppose I must say, Good-night
darling, God Bless you and may all
your dreams be pleasant Good luck.
    Au-revoir hope to see you soon
x   All my love to you forever
x x   x x   ~ Your ever loving wifey
x x x x x x x x x   x x x x x x Rene

June 14, 1946

My Darling Nick,
Many thanks sweetheart for the two letters I got this afternoon.
I hope this finds you okay darling as it leaves me but very very
lonely for a certain handsome guy who by the way happens to be
my husband (the best in all the whole wide world). I have a bit
of good news for you to-night darling. Doris got her papers this
morning and very short notice she has to be ready at 24hour notice
from to-morrow. I reckon the papers have been held up because
of the holidays. Her number is 38,616 so soon please God you can
look out for your little wifey, after them telling me at the repat
office yesterday they had reached 38,600 I knew Doris would hear
very soon. Now I know it's near the waiting seems worse then
ever, I can't sleep at all these nights. Last night I thought I would
go crazy, tossing and turning there, I think it's all the excitement.
I am glad you are getting on with the sink darling and that you
have made it special low for me, I think you are a real angel for
trying to get everything done, but please don't worry yourself too
much darling about everything. I am sure everything will work
out lovely especially if we are to-gether to figure it all out, with
you beside me darling I shan't care about a darn thing. The only
thing I worry about is that I hope I get used to everything quick-
ly because I know a lot of things are different over there to here.
One thing I know I musn't ask for a joint in the butcher. I don't
mind a bit about your teeth darling, you'll always be good-look-
ing and I shall love you in fifty years time just as much as I do, by
the way darling I didn't marry you for your looks, but you sure
are handsome. Casanova, I'm sorry I couldn't resist that. By the
way darling, is our house nearer to the factory than your mothers
was? I can just see you now some of these mornings, P.G. soon
jumping out of bed and dashing round so as you won't be late in
the morning, I guess that will be one of my wifely jobs, eh! Well
sweetheart I guess that's the news for another night, much as it
is, but it won't be long now darling, whoopee, when I can stop

writing to you I shall be the happiest girl in the world, but I thank God that we started writing nearly two years ago darling. Now I suppose I must say, Good-night darling, God Bless You and may all your dreams be pleasant. Good Luck. Au-revoir. Hope to see you soon. All my love to you forever.
Your ever loving wifey.
Rene

I LOVE YOU (in x's)

June 23, 2013

Dear Grama,
It comes with mixed emotions for me to tell you that my journey that has been structured around your letters has come to an end. You wrote your final letter to your sweetheart on June 23, 1946 and I've officially been through each and every one of the 110 letters that were scripted with love. There is a questionable gap between the date of the last letter and the date on the infamous telegram sent with excitement to Papa upon hearing the news of your sail date. That is something that I'll never have an answer to. Why the gap? Were the last few weeks of letters lost, thrown away, or never written at all? Does it even really matter?

Where I stand with it all in this very moment is that it was all part of the plan for me. Even before organizing the letters by date, I was invited to join a group of writers from the University of Windsor. I leave this Friday for France before leaving for my highly anticipated voyage home. I can't even begin to imagine what it will feel like to board that ship then depart on the 20 hour train journey to Windsor, just as you did. Over these last few weeks I've come to some deep and life changing realizations about my journey. The kind of realizations that keep me up at night writing. The time I've spent here living this dream truly has changed my life and it's incredible to think that it all began on a sunny day in California. So the rest of the journey's in my hands now as it truthfully has been since day one.

Thank you for such an incredible gift that brought me so much joy, clarity and adventure over these past 6 months. And you better believe that I will write often.

With a granddaughter's love & admiration,
Carly
xox

CHAPTER 21

A POSTCARD FROM PARIS

When I accepted Marty's offer to join a group of creative writing and photojournalist students for a summer course in France, I was honoured and a bit nervous. Not only did he invite me to take part in the course itself, but he also asked me to do my own talk for the group. So much happened between meeting Marty before leaving for London and stepping off the train in Burgundy. I couldn't wait to share my experience with his class and to learn from Marty and the other writers he brought with him to France.

On the second night of the course, it was my turn to present. I created a slideshow of photos from my journey, shared stories of tracing family history and experience across time, and talked about what I had learned about writing, myself, and my grandmother along the way.

My presentation was a hit. I shared it all, the good, the bad, and the *ugly*. I had the fellow writers laughing and for a few moments crying. I shared stories of the ups and downs of putting my hopes and dreams out there for the world to see and talked about what the creative process was like for me. I wrote every single day while in England, that in itself was quite the process. I showed them the picture I had taken of myself ugly crying because of self-doubt and loneliness, I shared what it was like to hear negative comments about myself in the media, the continual fear of pressing ENTER after writing a blog post, and the exhilaration that comes from doing something so different and unexpected and unplanned. I talked about the toll the trip took on friendships, my bank account, my time, and my career. And the *power* that comes from following a calling. I told them about meeting Brownie Dene and the power of connection and life stories. I explained that staying open and saying yes to these experiences had led me exactly where I needed to go. I was learning to be open with the writing process too, and it all came back to Marty's great advice: Write every single day about what you hear, see, and feel.

I loved sharing the lessons and insights I had learned on my journey with others. I loved hearing about their writing dreams and wanted to instill in them the courage to take up *their* call.

The rest of the time in France was filled with inspirational talks from authors, professors, creatives, and artists. We had time to write and reflect and take in the natural beauty around us on the century old farm that we stayed on. We enjoyed long outdoor French cuisine meals that lasted for hours and always ended with the most delicious cheese. And of course sightseeing, wine tasting, and an obligatory two-day trip to Paris.

June 30, 2013

Dear Grama,

Just a quick postcard to tell you what a lovely time I've been having in the enchanting city of Paris. I've spent time wandering the book and art stalls along the Seine stealing glances at Notre-Dame in between. I've spent an afternoon at cafes with colourful canopies and outward facing seats so the patrons can watch the world go by. I've wandered uphill to Montmarte taking in the picturesque rod-iron terraces lined with wooden shutters and flower boxes. The historical beauty of Paris is incredible and I've been officially swept off my feet by the love and romance that radiates from this city.

I was also sure to visit the one and only Eiffel Tower that literally made me jump up and down with excitement when it came into sight. As we climbed up to get the best view of the breathtaking structure, I once again lined myself up to the exact place that you stood many years before. I thought of the beauty of that moment and how there may be decades between the photographs but there was a bridge of understanding now that I hadn't had when I first started this trip. This photo of you was taken at a time that you and Papa had been reunited for many years, it was a trip you two did with a group of war-brides that you travelled the world with, and it was just a teeny, tiny glimpse of your happily ever after. It fills me with love, hope & gratitude.

With a granddaughter's love & admiration,
Carly
Xoxo

CHAPTER 22

LEAVING LONDON

I returned to London for my last week there, and I was overjoyed to be greeted by a familiar face from home. My co-worker Victoria and her Irish boyfriend Ed had been staying in my flat while I was in France. As soon as I got in, they handed me 10 handwritten letters from Adam that had arrived while I was away. I was so happy. It was such a beautiful evening that we decided to go to a park, and we stopped at a shop on the way to grab some fruit and wine. While they savoured the wine, I savoured every single word Adam had written. Reading his letters made me feel closer to him than I ever had before, even though we were still separated by miles. I was counting the days. I could not wait to see him.

A few days before I left London, Genevieve asked me to go swimming with her at the Hampstead Heath women's pond. Before this invitation, I'd never thought about swimming in a pond, let alone with only women. Part of the reason I never thought about it is because I can't really swim. I'd been so excited to see a women's swimming pond, which sounded all romantic and whimsical, that I'd forgotten all about the small fact that I'm not a swimmer. I was fairly certain that if my life depended on it I could, through some weird, ungraceful combination of leg kicking and arm flailing, save myself. But it would in no way resemble what most people think of as swimming.

I wondered if there was a connection between swimming and writing. I felt like what I was doing on my blog was akin to flailing my arms and legs in hopes that I could stay afloat. Every time I thought about writing a book, I froze. I'd been paddling around in the writing wading pool, posting to my weekly blog called *Life's*

Letter, but when I sat down to write "the book" the computer screen looked like a massive lake. No matter what I did, I couldn't seem to make myself jump in. Isn't life in general like this? Marriage. Raising babies. Pursuing careers. Aren't we all just learning as we jump in and embrace the fear?

The idea of a women-only swimming pond seemed both odd and cool at the same time. I envisioned the paintings I'd seen in museums of women bathing, mixed with goddess images that occasionally showed up on friends' Facebook pages. Genevieve told me that women had been coming to this private spot to swim in one of the ponds since the 1900s. We followed the winding tree-sheltered trail to a gate with a sign that read "No Men Beyond This Point."

Inside the changing house, pictures of women enjoying the peace and tranquility of a swim in the pond lined the walls. Outside, the temperature was freezing. I started to have second thoughts and then I saw a woman around 70 jump in. I watched in awe, as 50 years seemed to melt from her as she glided through the water. What was *I* waiting for?

As I moved towards the water, I thought about the letter my grandmother wrote about staying away from crowds. It seemed so out of character for her to be afraid of anything. The Grama I knew was bold, audacious, and fearless. The fears she faced and the tragedies she knew were unfathomable to my generation. I had been in high school when 9/11 happened, and I was in college when the London train bombings happened. While I was aware of how scary they were, they really didn't impact my everyday life like the war did my grandmother's. For six years, everyone in her world worried that Germany would invade England, they worried about all the young men they knew who were fighting, and they worried about what would happen to the families whose husbands, brothers, and sons didn't return home. They faced long separations, rationing, and an ongoing stream of bad news followed by funerals, occasionally punctuated by joyous announcements of a wedding or the cry of a newborn baby. When they heard the shriek of sirens signaling bombers overhead, they ducked into air-raid shelters. When they got the all clear, they returned to the dance hall where they fell in love with a soldier who would head off to war the next day. Not to mention the fact that my grandmother was Jewish. Had she been born in any other country, things would have been different. Things could have been like Lola, the holocaust survivor I had met and befriended at the bank...if she was lucky.

My fears seemed so small in comparison. The fear of being in London alone. Of occasionally feeling lonely. The fear of putting my words and dreams out for all to see. The fear of not being able to write a book and make something meaningful come from this journey.

One of the lessons I'd worked on the entire time I was in England was to see life through my grandmother's eyes. To, as she had, face fear rather than run from it. To embrace the ambiguity that life offered up in place of certainty. And to jump into the pond, rather than hang at the side of the pond and let my fear of not being able to swim stop me. I jumped in. The minute I was in the water I was enveloped with a calm so deep I knew it came from her. And I realized that much of the discontentment I'd been feeling was because I'd felt so disconnected from everything – Adam, my family, my friends, home. But there, gliding around the pond, perhaps for the first time in months, I was present. I wasn't worrying about the next day or the next week or the week after that. All I was focused on was the feeling of the water as it rippled past me, the smells around me, and the glorious sense of being fully and completely in the moment.

Letters only tell us part of the story. From what my mother told me and from conversations I remember having with my grandfather, my grandmother learned to embrace her fears. She found adventure in the events of her day, even when other people were running away from them. She even found sleeping in the Swiss Cottage tube station during the air raids exciting. Yes, occasionally she shied away, but most of the time she embraced life. She threw herself into life in Canada. She built a life there, while at the same time holding on to her British roots.

Floating around the pond, I thought about the relationship between fear and time. Fear pulls us out of the present and either takes us back to a day, month, or year in the past, filling us with regret and sorrow about what we didn't do, or it takes us into the future and fills us with dread about what is to come and the worry of whether or not we can handle it. When I think back over the fears that plagued me in those months I'd been in London, in my past relationships, throughout my life, none of them seemed founded. Certainly none of them had really done any good. If anything, they got in the way of what it was I was doing. When I looked back on fears, what I saw were missed opportunities to run towards the excitement and seek out the joy that life has to offer. And I vowed that that was exactly what I was going to do.

For me, the ponds at Hampstead Heath were a sacred place. I had an awakening there. The Mumford & Sons song "Awake My Soul" became my new theme song and the line from the song, "In this body we will live, in this body we will die...where you invest your love, you invest your life" became my new mantra.

I thanked Genevieve for sharing the space with me. A space that changed me and gave me such amazing perspective and clarity. And I silently thanked my Grama for showing me the way.

On my last day in London, I wrote Adam a final letter. For the first time in my life, I knew what I wanted. I wanted Adam. I wanted to marry him and have children with him someday. I wanted to travel with him and fall in love with him every day for the rest of our lives. I wanted to fall asleep beside him and wake up next to him. I wanted to buy our first house together, decorate it, and make it a special place for our family and friends. I wanted to have BBQs and go on holidays together. I wanted to face whatever life had in store for us, the good times and the bad, with Adam by my side. I wanted to get home to him and tell him all the things I'd learned that were impossible to write in letters and to see his face as I shared the tiny details of the trip that *he* had encouraged me to take.

July 18, 2013

Hey babycakes,
Oh I had the most magical day today. I made my rounds and said goodbye to everyone at the Italian café. Niko, the owner, said he'd keep an eye out for my book. I stopped by at 21 Fairfax one last time to say farewell to the house itself and to drop off a card for Renee to thank her for that pleasant first meeting with you back in January. It truly did start my journey off in the most magical way. I then made my way to say goodbye to Brownie Dene, the 93 year old who I met in Regent's Park in the Queen Mary Garden way back when. I found her place right near Russell Square but she wasn't home when I first went. I went to a café to finish a few letters. I thought I'd try one last time and she was home. I had a card and photo of us for her and she invited me in. We had cupcakes and tea as she shared stories and photographs of her time in the theatre. We talked about you and our wed-

ding, my Grama, and my book. We talked about France, my journey, what it was like to meet her, and what kind of an impact it had on me. I was so lonely that day we first met and she reminded me so much of Grama and brought me so much comfort. When I told the story of meeting her in France, that was what had people crying. I told her that and she thanked me for sharing and couldn't believe she had that kind of impact. We talked about what name she wants me to give her in the book and she said, "You can absolutely call me Brownie Dene! Keep her alive!"

She wants us to send her a wedding photo of us and she wants to be pen pals. She said that she considers me family. I don't think she has a lot of family around. I really want to keep in touch with her. I then went to leave and she expressed just how happy she was for me. She said it was so lovely to hear such joyful things in one life and honey... It's so true! I'm so blessed. We are so blessed. This is so true that it could make me cry. I feel like the luckiest gal in the world to have you, health, amazing parents, in-laws (to-be), and oh I could go on and on and on. We are so lucky. Like Jessica's Affirmations on YouTube, I love my whole HOUSE (and we don't even have one yet). We had the loveliest visit and it truly meant the world to her to have me there.

I was pretty high on life after that, and as I was wandering, trying to find Russell Square, I had this overwhelming feeling that I had been here before. It felt so familiar and I had a feeling the hotel we stayed at in 1995 was around this area. I got a little lost, kept wandering and sure enough went around the corner to see: The Royal National Hotel. It made me think about my 10-year-old self that stood in that very spot all those years ago and the life and adventure that lay before her. I smiled and knew it was Grama bringing me back to where my story with England all began. I remembered exactly where our room was and what view we had. I wandered the streets and actually remembered the first time I was there. As I walked into the courtyard of the hotel, I stopped for a picture. As I looked down to put my camera away, there at my feet was a 20p coin. Thanks Grama.

I then made my way down to Central London to say goodbye to Harry at the theatre and gave him his card and printed out blog post that I wrote about him. I then had takeaway sushi at a park then did my favourite walk one last time. Leicester Square, Trafalgar Square, South Bank, the Eye, and crossed Westminster Bridge. I had one last date with my boyfriend Ben...who dinged at 10pm with all of his might (sorry I'm just telling you about him now) and had some cadbury chocolate buttons as I stared up into his (clock) face shining down on me. (Don't worry, you're way more handsome!)

Oh honey...this is it. I'll be home so so soon. I know it's been crazy but think of how lovely it will be to be in your arms again. I'm so excited. I feel like I have so much to thank you for.

Thank you for messaging me after I sang with Matt.
Thank you for taking me on a date in your dad's truck.
Thank you for showing up on my doorstep before California.
Thank you for being you and letting me fall in love with you.
Thank you for being patient with me to tell you.
Thank you for falling in love with me (hair drama and all!).
Thank you for not running when you heard about England.
Thank you for your support since day one.
Thank you for asking me to marry you.
Thank you for loving me.
And even with all of these Thank You's, it doesn't feel like

it does it justice.
How about I'll show you in a few short days.
I love you,

Carly
Xo

Jess and Ollie came to see me off the night before my departure and to have a few farewell drinks. One turned into two, and the tubes had run their last route so they ended up crashing on the floor and were stuck with me. Maybe not the best choice during a rare English heatwave with two extra humans in my teeny tiny flat, but thank goodness, because I was a stress case when we all woke up and they lovingly helped push me out the door to catch my bus. I had 10 pounds to my name, mostly coins that I had found from Grama, and I couldn't find my metro card, but off I went.

As far as my very last letter to Adam on British soil, I realized early that morning that I had overcommitted by thinking that the day of sailing would have any downtime to write and find a post-box. I had numbered the envelopes months in advance, and when the time came on the last day to send the envelope with the number 1 penned on it, I knew that I needed to hand it over. Because my packing had turned into a bit of a frenzy and the celebrations the night before were more than anticipated, as I said my goodbyes to Ollie and Jess, I handed them the envelope and asked them to fill it with a letter and mail it off to Adam.

It wasn't until two years later that I sat down and read their words:

Hello Adam,
As you can probably tell by my awful handwriting that this isn't your lover Carly, it's Ollie! I hope you're doing well on the other side of the pond. I admire your support in Carly

and I understand how you must be feeling. It was very tough for me and Jess when we started as all you want is that person to be with you. But then that was just how it was as we both lived in separate countries, where as your daft Carly chose to do this! That to me is both mad and tough, but also what I've learnt is very worthwhile and important. I can tell how much Carly has got from this but also it's shown to her and us how much you mean to her. No doubt you're feeling the same. So as I said, I admire you both for choosing to put yourself through this. It's not easy and I know it's not nice (at times).

Anywho, enough of that deep lovey dovey bollox. The main news is that Carly is on her way home to you now. We had a great last night in London with her. Jess helped her finish packing and then they went out to a close by Café, where they both overindulged in wine and hummus. Soon after I joined them I tried to catch up in the beers. It was a nice evening so we sat outside and chatted as we half paid attention to the world go by. After a bottle of wine and my two beers, we agreed it was time to eat a kebab. As Willesden Green has a high population of Turkish residence, this wasn't the hardest plan to execute! We trusted Carly's choice and we were not let down. However, we ate in instead of getting it to take away. My kebab was served on a plate with a side of salad and red cabbage. Not what I had in mind (being a tasty wrap with spicy & garlic sauce) but it was still delightful and sufficed microwave. We headed back for Carly's as we had lost track of time and also the last tube home. We stayed over (girls in the bed, me on the floor) and just passed out instantly. I could tell Carl's was feeling nervous about the journey the next day. So I double checked with her what the plan was and what would be enough time to wake up and leave. The plan was set so we quietly spoke about the boat and how exciting it was. And of course about your good self and how much she loves you.

Morning came and we all felt slightly jaded and fluffy from the night of booze and posh kebabs. Naturally Carly was more nervous and started pottering around not actually doing anything while mumbling something about stress. Me and Jess talked her down and through everything. We helped pack her last bits and we also had our bags of goodies that she was leaving for us too. Soon it was all good and we were out the door. Carly freaked about how many bags she had to carry and tried to convince us to carry them to the bus stop for her (Princess Carly)! We declined as we had our own bags of goodies, but helped her put bags into bags, and balance them on top. The final hug goodbye came and there were tears. She lingered and paused so I said, "Turn around and fuck off!" She giggled out loud and walked across the road. The last I heard Carly say back was, "Thanks for everything guys, bye. I'm getting a taxi!" We all burst into laughter and went our separate ways. Jess was feeling very down after that so I hope you know that Jess will be very jealous of you now. Sorry for the long letter. I only meant to say hi. Well we're coming over to Canada soon too so we'll be able to have a proper catch up over a beer or six. I'm really looking forward to it. All the best my friend and please give Carly a big hug from both of us too. All the love to you and your family too.

Cheers,

Ollie

Hello Adam!!!

Carly is officially off on a boat back to her beloved fiancée (that's you!) and I really don't think she could be more excited! We had a great last night send off in London town. Ollie and I met up with Carly after work in her hood. We were

going to go to the Queensberry but sat at a little weird café for the night, just down the road from her flat. (Well, actually first Carly and I went to her flat to finish packing because she was panicking, haha, but then we went to the café and met Ollie there). Before Ollie got there, Car and I had a lovely chat about her time in London, what's coming up next, and obviously about you and how excited she is to build a life with you. Honestly Adam, in the decade of knowing Carly as a best friend (lucky me!!) I've NEVER seen her this content, sure, happy and ... what's the word I'm looking for ... I guess serene. I mean, she's obviously still a crazy nut, but when it comes to her relationship with you, it's just magic to be an outsider looking in at. Anyways, suffice it to say, we drank too much wine, became best friends with our waiter Reggie, had a kebab from "Woody's Grill," then fell asleep for the night. In the morning, Carly was panicking again, but I was a bit too hung over to be any help, so Ollie took over and bossed her around a bit, it was great, haha! We sent her on her way, overloaded with suitcases and a sad little cry of, "I need Adam!" when we asked how she was going to carry it all, again, we laughed! It was such a wonderful pleasure getting to have your fiancé in the same city with me for six months, and as much as I had a few tears having to say goodbye, I couldn't be happier that she's on her way back to you! So glad you've come into our lives you furry thing :)
See you soon!

Jess

CHAPTER 23

QUEEN MARY II

July 20, 2013
Bus from Victoria Coach Station - Southampton
DEPARTS 9:30 am - 11:45 am
Board Queen Mary II - noon - DEPARTS - 3:00 pm

    As I kicked off my sandals, leaned back, and stretched out onto
the wooden deck chair, I took a deep breath in and let out a sigh
of relief. I made it. I was onboard the Queen Mary II. This moment
right here marked the beginning of my voyage home. With every
sailing day, I would come that much closer to my happily ever after

with Adam. I took a big swig of my ice-cold lemonade and felt it make its way down my throat. It might have been the first thing I had to drink that whole day.

And what a day it was. Travel days always were for me. Especially when I had to do it alone. I pulled out the Queen Mary stationery I had grabbed from my stateroom desk after quickly dropping off my bag and beelining it to Deck 7 to get a good seat for departure. I wanted to watch the dock as we sailed away to ensure that I had a view of England until it was out of sight. I wanted to let it all sink in and reflect on what it must have been like for my Grama as she bid her beloved country goodbye this way 67 years earlier on the original Queen Mary with the other war brides on their way to their new life, new homes, and new husbands.

Dearest Darling,

Today was my first day on the Queen Mary. Oh, it is so magical. One thing that's for sure is that you would love it...especially the king sized bed. They've pushed two twins together, but I'll most likely just use the one side. My day of traveling here started bright and early. I was a little stressed and let's be honest: a hot mess – as you can probably recall from back in January before we left.

Once I finally got everything sorted: garbage out, stuff for Ollie and Jess, stuff for Sophia, stuff for the charity shop and stuff I was bringing with me, then I could at least breathe a little. The breathing didn't last too long because I was carrying two small suitcases, a purse, my camera bag, a dress bag on a hanger, and a shopping bag. Ugh my body is so weak. I need you babe. And not just to carry my things either. I need you in EVERY way possible.

After I got on the first bus after saying goodbye to Jess and

Ollie through the tears, I fumbled and stumbled my way on with a pretty loud, "Oh Shit!"for all the passengers to hear when my bag fell forward and created a big Carly Shit Show scene. When I got to Victoria Station there was construction, of course, so I ended up having to schlep my stuff probably about a mile out of the way after all was said and done. Once I got to the coach station though, I was golden and so ready to sit. There was a bit of traffic on the motorway on the way to Southampton but it all disappeared from my memory the second the bright red twin funnels came into sight. I think I actually made a gasping noise out of excitement.

Due to the previous schlepping nightmare, even though I could literally see the Queen Mary from the bus stop I decided to get a taxi and get dropped off right in front of the loading docks. A man met me as I came out of the cab to offer to take my luggage. "Absolutely," I accepted with a smile. As I put the luggage tags on my bags, which I totally should have done before arriving at the docks, he asked if I was travelling alone. After saying yes, he told me what a brave young lady I was. I gotta be honest that I sort of love hearing that after all this time. I got myself all checked in, through security and onto the ship at long last! Oh, the Queen Mary sure is spectacular. I got into my stateroom, hung my dresses and made my way to the upper deck. It was a gorgeous sunny day so I snapped some pictures of its beauty. I then went to a mandatory safety drill to learn about the lifejackets and lifeboats and then we were all set to sail.

There was a big send off party going on at the front of the ship, so I went to get some free champagne that ended up not being free at all. I decided to opt for the free lemonade and now I'm sitting on the lounge chairs on Deck 7 where

I sat while we sailed away from the harbour. I met some nice folks our parents' age and enjoyed the sailboats going by as we blew our whistle upon departure. It was magical and it made me think about what it must have been like for Grama. The sound of the whistle alone must have filled her whole soul with excitement.

I can't believe I'm here, babe, finally at last on my way home to you. Thank you for being so supportive of this adventure, my love. I couldn't have done any of this without you.
Love you,

Carly
Xoxo

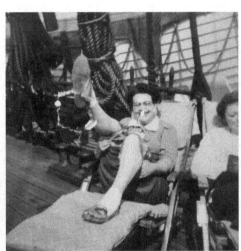 

Grama and Carly aboard the Queen Mary

The Queen Mary II sure was majestic. From the sweeping staircases to the vaulted stained glass ceiling and elegant dining room. There was an indoor pool with pouring fountains. Afternoon tea was served in the Queen's dining room. Shakespeare and other stage productions were available in the evening, as well as author talks, painting classes, and lectures. I felt so fancy getting dressed up for dinners every night. I checked out a few shows here and there and peeked in on the dance halls in the evenings. In reality though, it was way out of my league, and as beautiful as it was, all I wanted to do was relax, eat good food, write in my journal, and watch every sunset. Similar to my time in England, the people I met on board the Queen Mary quickly became a highlight of the journey.

Almost everyone I met started with some sort of curious line about what on earth had brought a 30-something-year-old lone traveller on a seven-day ocean liner across the Atlantic. I was assigned to the early dinner to a table of lone travellers, those traveling without a partner or companion. While the concierge got the lone traveller part right, they must not have checked my age. I was at least 30 and in some cases 60 years younger than anyone at my table.

Seated at my table was Veronika, a 91-year-old Holocaust survivor from Poland who was wise and kind and full of grandmotherly advice.

Peter was an accountant, who appeared to be in his 60s. He reminded me of my crazy uncle. One minute he was telling a joke or funny story, and the next, he was storming out of the dining room because it had become entirely too noisy. He confessed that he was a homebody and that he really didn't like people. Why he had chosen to go on a cruise remained a mystery.

And there was Tal, a Persian from NYC. She was great. She loved talking about all things Oprah, the power of positive thinking, and our shared love for travel and New York City.

There were two other women who had retired from banking, but we didn't see much of them. They spent most of the time finagling places at the captain's table. On one of the rare meals we

Carly on Deck 7

spent together, they told me if they had been my boss at the bank, they would have never approved my leave of absence! Their advice was to go back to the bank and stay there and work my way up so that I could buy a big home and a nice car, go on a bunch of cruises, and then I'd be set, like them. I was happy for them, but that sure wasn't my dream.

With every conversation, I felt like my grandmother wasn't finished guiding me yet. She wanted me to continue to hear other people's stories. To connect to them and to learn from them. What she couldn't teach me personally she made sure I got through the connections I made, and I cherished each one.

Sunset soon became my favourite time of day onboard. Every night, I would walk along Deck 7, looking for the perfect spot to take in the gorgeous view, and on one particular night, I decided on a lounge chair next to a man I had crossed paths with a few times before. This was the first time we had a conversation, though. At first, it was polite small talk exchanged between strangers but quickly turned into one of the most meaningful connections I had made onboard. His name was James, and he was from just outside of London. After talking for 15 minutes about where we were from, what brought us here, and what we did for a living, we started talking about the real stories of our lives, the ones that make us unique, make us whole, and make us, us. Just as the real conversation started, he got up and moved seats to get a better view of the sunset. It seemed as if he was getting more comfortable and continued to talk while looking out at sea, not turning to look back at me much. It's as if we went from chitchat to the therapist's chair. I could almost see the comfort he felt as he started getting into his life story.

"My experience of the war was a little different than your gran's. I was only a boy at the time and was actually sent out of London as a child evacuee," he explained. Until this moment on the ship's deck under the stars, I honestly hadn't even thought about what it must have been like for the younger generations during the war. It was an aspect of the war that I was hearing about for the first time.

"I was 4 years old and put onboard a train heading out of London. I stayed in Yorkshire with a wonderful lady I called "Me Mum", because she really was like a second mother to me. I considered it an adventure as a 4 year old and once I got out of the station, "Me Mum" came up to me, and said she'd be taking me home to look after me and that it was all going to be okay. She was lovely to me and I had a great four years with her and her children."

He paused as his eyes seemed locked on the horizon, but in another place.

"Way too many years passed, and me and my family went to see her. She kept looking over at me, almost staring."

As he got tears in his eyes, he said, "All I wanted to do was go over and hug her, but I didn't. I regret it deeply as that was the last time I saw her. It just felt so strange because my wife and family was there with me and she had hers. A few years later at her funeral, her granddaughter told me that "Me Mum" never got over losing me at 8 years old. It was tough on her, and she had deep sadness around that."

Nearly 100,000 children were evacuated from London during

the war, an event that impacted lives of the children, their biological parents, and the receiving families who opened up their homes. I tried to imagine the emotions of the parents shipping off their children, or the kids themselves, or the new caregivers welcoming and loving another parent's child, only to lose them years later when the war ended.

"Before we were evacuated, I remember being in Camden during the air raids, hanging out in the longest, deepest fire escape in London. Myself and the other kids hid in there, in between running to the British museums and sneaking into the cinemas. We would hire rowboats for what was supposed to be an hour that we would use for the whole day. I remember what it was like to see cars and trucks for the first time in London. On one occasion, we went on a trip to my Gran's in London near Camden and were amazed at what seemed to be real life Tonka trucks driving around. Her house had been bombed, and I remember seeing the curtains fluttering in the wind and how the whole front of the house had been hit. We found her sitting in her armchair reading the paper, as if nothing had happened. During one of the air raids, my garden got hit by an M2, and I remember hearing the whistle of it coming down, and all of a sudden the noise stopped as it dropped. It killed five of my chickens, and a whole block of flats was destroyed. Many people around me lost their lives during that time. We really were lucky to be alive. And we were so thankful for the Canadian soldiers who were the first to come to England's aid."

I felt a sense of pride for not only my country but for my grandfather as well. James was in the Air Force for a while himself, but didn't seem to want to talk much about that. He spoke of travelling all over Europe after "packing it in" with his stock market job and wondered if he would have been a millionaire had he stayed. We contemplated it for a minute, and we both agreed that rich in money and rich in experiences are much different.

I love when conversations go to this place, and I felt honoured to witness someone opening up about their life story. It's the kind of connection that gives me chills and makes me aware that this is what life is all about. If it was a love letter I could write to someone, it would say: Share your life story. I'm here to listen. You deserve to tell it. You are worthy. You are heard.

I thanked and acknowledged him for sharing his story with me, not only because it was fascinating to hear about the impact the war had on him, but also the fact that it is dear to him and takes a lot for someone to open up like that. It was an honour to have met him. Before he stood up to leave, we exchanged mailing addresses and promised to keep in touch.

As I sat to take in a few more minutes to myself, I started to feel lonely and missed Adam with every bone in my body. It made me think of Grama on the ship missing Papa, feeling so close yet so far away. Although being on the ship itself was exciting and interesting, I couldn't help but feel a little sad. I tried to stay positive and remind myself how lucky I was that he had been so supportive since day one and tried to shift my mind to a place of gratitude that he was in my life to miss. I also noticed the anxiety I felt about going home. It was interesting because I was feeling things slowly on this voyage, being a gradual, seven-day trip home. Had I hopped on a flight, everything would have been more instant and shocking, waking up in a different place and being in a new country and time zone in a matter of hours. Every day onboard, we lost an hour, which really made me feel a sense of completion and closure to the journey.

There was also anxiety about the book writing process, going back to work, not having any money, and feeling doubts about whether I had done this all right. Part of me knew that there was no right and wrong way to do a self-designed quest, but since day one it had been a constant question in my mind. As I walked past Winter's Garden to head to bed, I heard the melody of the piano dance through the air. The familiar tune of "Somewhere Over the Rainbow" rang true in my mind and made me feel a deep sense of relief. I was here, I had made it, and everything was as it should be.

The next morning was a rocky one. The waves were so rough that the outside decks were closed for most of the day. The most important thing was finding big windows to plop myself in front of. Being able to see the horizon helped with the motion. Michael, who I had met in the laundromat on the second day onboard, stopped to say hello as he walked by. He was a teacher from Texas, originally from Japan. After our initial conversation over folded laundry, he went back to tell his family about my journey. He was so thrilled to run into me again, because he wanted to share that his 8-year-old son was on a similar journey himself. Michael's wife's father had taken a ship over the Atlantic from Ireland to Canada eventually making their way to Halifax with his mom when he was 8. So his 8-year-old boy was doing a similar journey to one his grandfather took decades before. It was pretty neat to think that there was someone else connecting to their family story on the very same ship. We talked about getting to know our parents and grandparents as people. Michael had a pretty life-changing experience after his father's death, finding out that his dad was previously married to a young girlfriend, who at the time, told him she was pregnant. It made me think about how my mom and I found out through the letters that my grandfather was engaged to someone back home before leaving for the war.

We talked about having kids, and his advice was to enjoy some married life just the two of us first. He told me that things really change when babies are in the picture, and it's important to build yourselves as a unit first. Before leaving, he told me what a brave, bold, adventurous, and courageous thing I was doing, which made me think of Grama. That is exactly what I think of her and what she did, so it was pretty cool to hear that people were seeing that in me, too.

I went back to my stateroom and got ready for our final dinner onboard. I tried on two dresses before settling on the red dress with white polka dots, the one I was sure Grama would have loved.

I always tried to snag a seat next to Veronika because she spoke quietly with a thick Polish accent. She lived in Florida and had been travelling since April. She explained how cruising was a perfect way for her to travel because she was unable to fly for more than three hours due to her heart condition. I just knew that she had some stories to share, and I wanted a front row seat. After the first course, she got into the story of her life, and I was captivated by the first word. She was a 90-year-old Holocaust survivor and was put into concentration camps for nine months. She was liberated by the army and then moved to London, where she lived for 20 years. When she was in London, she lived near Victoria Station about a 10-minute walk from Buckingham Palace. She told me about her trips that she took back to Poland every year and about staying with her life-long friend that she had for 60 years.

Dinner was lovely. Once the two bankers left for their captain's party, the four of us had such fascinating conversations. We talked about how nice it was to meet one another. Peter quickly explained at the beginning of dinner that his reason for leaving so abruptly the night before was an urgent need for the bathroom – at least that's his story and he's sticking to it. He went on playfully calling me a flighty young lady, teased me about not being able to cook, and referred to me as Henry all night. I told him that he reminds me of my uncle, so I started calling him Uncle Peter. Tal and I really got to bond earlier in the day at the champagne bar, talking for two hours about life, signs from the universe, and listening to your calling.

As we hugged goodbye after that final dinner together, we bid one another farewell and all the luck in the future. As we were going around the table, Veronika then called me an unusual young lady with charm and wonder and a creative mind. She told me to take care of myself and gave me some advice to take care of Adam because no matter how manly a husband is, they all want to be taken care of. She told me to let him know often – although not too often – just how much I appreciate him. She told me to enjoy the happiness and to keep in touch. When she was talking about Adam, I felt quite emotional and had tears in my eyes.

Peter wished me well in my future and told me that he hopes to meet my children someday. As he hugged me goodbye, he quietly told me to walk Veronika to her room. A little confused as to where that came from, I took his advice and obliged. As we slowly made our way to her room, she went on to tell me more of her story. She told me about her husband dying five years ago and how he died at home while holding her hand in their bed. She told me about the really hard time she had with it and how angry she was with God. She talked to her priest about it, and he helped her eventually see that this was only her point of view and that God really did give her husband a gift by giving him the gift of rest, dying in his own home, and going peacefully without suffering. He worked hard all his life and needed rest. She talked about how nice it feels to think about being able to be with him again someday in heaven. She said logically it doesn't make complete sense, but it helps her feel better. We talked about bringing Adam to visit in Sarasota and that she would arrange a place for us to stay.

She told me about the friends and group activities that she does at home, reading Shakespeare, and how before this, she would never read it aloud because of her accent. She told me about her niece who's a nurse and an artist.

We both had tears in our eyes when she told me what a special person I was and how happy she was for me and Adam. She said, "I really hope he is worthy of you." I started to tear up again and assured her that he absolutely was and that she'll be able to attest to it when she gets to meet him.

As I made my way back to my stateroom, holding back the tears as best as I could, I flopped onto the bed and sobbed. It was all sinking in finally...everything that I was trying to access this whole time had been right at my fingertips. It was connection.

I grabbed some Kleenex and headed up to Deck 7. It was my last night on the ship, after all. I had to see what kind of sunset show was on tonight. As I opened the doors and got the first glance, I just knew there had to be some angels putting on an art show for us all to see. It was the most beautiful sunset I had ever seen. Maybe it was Grama, Veronika's husband, or "Me Mum." All I could do was smile.

CHAPTER 24

NEW YORK CITY

The ship arrived in New York City on July 27. The captain had told us that if we woke up around 4:30 am, we would be sailing under the bridge and then making our way towards the Statue of Liberty and Manhattan. Just as I stepped out the door onto Deck 7, we were approaching the bridge, which was all lit up in its glory. I snapped some pictures and gravitated towards the pink glow of the early morning sunrise. You could feel the anticipation in the air, and as the ship approached closer and closer, the crowd grew and the excitement continued. Seeing my dream city in this light from the deck of the Queen Mary made me love it even more. I felt like it was Grama saying, "Here you go, love. From one amazing city to another. We all know how much you love this place. Enjoy! This is your journey, after all."

I hurried in to have a shower and came out one last time to take some photos wearing my grandmother's scarf. In that moment, I realized this was exactly the way it was supposed to be. Ever since I was a kid, I always had a fascination with New York City. I had NYC posters on my wall, a Statue of Liberty trinket that my parents gave me in the 90s, and was forever doodling *I HEART NYC* with a cityscape skyline in my notebooks. I would prance around in my mom's high heels and use my Music For Young Children piano bag as a briefcase and pretend I was a businesswoman walking the streets of New York for a meeting. Despite my grandmother sailing into Halifax, there couldn't have been a more perfect location for me to sail into.

Sailing into New York wearing Grama's scarf

We disembarked and went through customs in an orderly fashion. We were some of the last ones off the ship, having been in the cheapest cabins onboard. I hopped in a cab with a couple I met in the cab line after dodging the sun as best I could. It was HOT in the city when we arrived, and I forgot to put sunscreen on. I went into Manhattan to a coffee shop to meet up with my dear friend Lisa and had a day of tourist fun in the city that never sleeps. Since the moment we met, we had been close friends. She was from Connecticut, but had lived in New York for years, so knew her way around and knew all the ins and outs of the city. As eager as I was to get home to Adam and my family, I loved that day in the city. Luckily, she had arranged for us to stay with her friends on the Upper West Side, so we were able to catch some z's before catching the train the next morning to Toronto.

Lisa joined me for the train voyage because I figured my grand-mother, at that point, after the long voyage on the Queen Mary, was bound to have made some friends that she rode the train with, so Lisa took the role as the fill-in fellow war bride. We took the train all the way from NYC to Toronto. Then the next morning from Toronto to Windsor. I was ending the journey exactly as my grandmother had all those years before. I would arrive in Windsor on the train, and just as my grandfather had been there to greet her, Adam would be too.

CHAPTER 25

TRAIN RIDE TO REUNITE

July 28, 2013

NYC (Penn Station) to Toronto

DEPART NY - 7:15 am on Maple Leaf (Amtrak) Train #63

ARRIVE at the New York Canadian border - 4:37 pm

DEPART Canadian Border - 4:57 pm on Maple Leaf Train #7098

ARRIVE - Toronto -7:42 pm - Union Station

July 29, 2013

VIA RAIL Train #73

DEPART Toronto 12:15 pm to ARRIVE in Windsor at 4:26 pm

The moment was everything I had imagined. As the train slowly rolled into the Windsor Train Station, I caught a glimpse of Adam out the window and had butterflies. He looked so handsome. I couldn't take my eyes off him as I waited for the train to stop and the door to open. I hadn't talked to him in so long. I was so nervous, it almost felt like I was meeting him for our first date all over again. I didn't really know what to do or say.

I stepped from the train and I literally jumped into his arms. I was home! Adam was my home and my future. If the last six months had taught me anything, it was that I did not want to be apart again any time soon.

Reuniting with Adam

That week was a flurry of seeing friends and family interrupted with follow-up media appearances on CTV and CBC. I spent the week anticipating the engagement party that Adam and my mom had arranged. It seemed like everyone we loved was going to be there. Elyse and Alec had moved back to Canada a few months prior, and even Jess and Ollie had flown over from England for a summer visit with her family. I was so excited to see them all again so soon.

It was odd to be back at home in the bedroom that I had grown up in. I hadn't lived in Leamington for 10 years. It felt comforting and familiar like home always did, while at the same time uncertain on how the transition would go settling back in town. Summers in South Western Ontario were the best time to be there. The air was hot and humid from the freshwater lakes, and the big open fields made for a sunset that you can see for miles. Our small town was known for its incredible sweet corn, Burgesses ice cream, and delicious field tomatoes that barreled by in the truckload on their way to Heinz. It helped that I had Lisa visiting to show the town off to. I got to see it all again with fresh eyes.

We spent part of the week touring the area wineries and hanging out at the beach. And while I was busy showing Lisa where I grew up, I noticed that Adam's family seemed very busy. I stopped by to show Adam's mom Pat, his sister Shannon, and sister-in-law Melissa my wedding dress. I was relieved that they loved it, but they seemed pretty preoccupied with all that needed to be done for the engagement party. They lovingly shooed me away so they could run errands that needed to be done before Saturday.

With the engagement party excitement in the air, my mom insisted that I try on her wedding dress just for fun to see if I could incorporate it into our May wedding in some way. It seemed a bit early to be thinking about it, but I humored her. Seeing the dress on, I thought about wearing it for the ceremony and the dress I bought in London for the reception. My dress still needed to be hemmed, and while I had it on, my mom decided to pin it so it could be altered. I tried to tell her not to bother, we had 10 months to worry about it, but she had always been one of those people who would rather get something done than put it off. Still I worried the pins would get rusty before I got around to taking the dress to the seamstress.

We talked about my mom and dad's wedding memories and then of course the stories we always heard about my grandparents' wedding. It was hard to believe that Papa needed to get permission from so many people to marry Grama. His family and the military didn't want him to marry her because she was Jewish, her family didn't want her to marry a Canadian soldier and leave

England, and the military chaplain had to sign off on it. They were originally supposed to be married on October 27 1945, but the choppy English Channel caused a delay to the 30, and they almost missed their date again on the 30 because the car broke down on the way to the wedding. We agreed that even with the wedding day mishaps and hoops they had to jump through to get married, their love was an inspiration.

The night before the engagement party, my dad had a concert down at the marina, which was nice timing for the out-of-town guests who had come in for the party. It would have been a perfect night, except that Adam wasn't there. I couldn't believe that he was working late on the night before our engagement party. And so soon after I got home. I tried not to be upset, but it was so unlike him.

Just as I was falling asleep that night, my dad knocked on my bedroom door. He came in and sat on the edge of my bed. He said, "I want you to know how much I love you." He was being really sentimental and quite adorable. I thought it was because he had missed me so much, or because we were having the engagement party the next day that would publically mark the beginning of my separation from my parents and joining Adam as his wife. I tried to see it from his point of view. His baby was about to celebrate her engagement to the man of her dreams. Maybe that was it. I thought, *Boy, if he is this emotional over the engagement, I can't imagine how he will be when I actually get married.*

Adam got in very late that night. I was already fast asleep. I vaguely remember waking up enough to kiss him goodnight.

CHAPTER 26

SURPRISE!

I woke up on the morning of our engagement party excited to share our day with all of our friends and family and to see people I hadn't seen during all the months I'd been away. I was determined to put aside all my aggravation at Adam's no-show the night before and how distracted he'd been since I'd gotten home. I rolled over to cuddle in close and steal a few moments before the big day, and realized I was in bed alone. Where the heck was Adam? He'd gotten in so late the night before, I was surprised he was already up and going.

A few minutes later, he came into my room and told me to throw on some clothes because he had a surprise for me. And then he rushed back out again. Okay, he really was acting odd.

When I joined him in the living room, I was surprised to see the videographer that we'd booked for our wedding with his camera out and ready to go. My first thought was, *What a lovely surprise! Adam has hired the videographer for the engagement party!* And then I thought, *Why is he here so early?*

Adam took my hand and led me to the couch. He sat down next to me and handed me a letter. Before I even started reading it, I was crying. Letters had become so important to me. They were symbols of journeys and change, growth and love, and now on the day of our engagement party Adam had given me the perfect gift – a letter.

He asked me to read the letter out loud. Nervous and a little teary I read:

Good morning Gorgeous,

This letter is slightly different from all the other letters I've written to you. For starters, I am standing in the same room as you right now. Hello. You're the best thing that has ever happened to me. You have changed my outlook on life for the better by just being your amazing self. I have never met anyone as brave as you are. Just last year you dreamed up what most people would consider a crazy idea and plan, and over the last 6 months we have lived it out. Amazing. The love I feel for you is indescribable, overwhelming, breathtaking and honest. There is no effort in loving you. It's like I was born to do it. Which leads me into what this letter is all about. For the last few months I have been planning an engagement party with several people, mainly your momma. To show and allow all of your friends and family to see us together engaged. Can you believe Elyse and Alec are the only people to see us together in real life engaged? We've been engaged for so long. I have missed you so much. But, what I'm trying to tell you is that today is not our engagement party, it is our wedding. Is your heart pounding? Because mine is. Today we are getting married in front of all of our family and friends. Today we start out as Mr. and Mrs. Verheyen. Take a deep breath my beautiful bride to be. Your mom and I have taken care of everything. I mean everything. Today I just want you to enjoy yourself, feel the love I have for you, laugh, smile, have fun. Your bridesmaids are on their way, your hairdresser is on her way, your makeup is on its way. You are completely taken care of. I love you so much and today we will show the world that we are together forever. I love you.

Love always,
Adam

We were getting married? Today? He had arranged *everything!?* Everyone I had booked was on the way – my hairdresser, the makeup artist, the photographer, and flowers – everything had been arranged. *What?*

Before the enormity of what was happening really hit me, both of our families came in. They were overjoyed and excited. Everyone just assumed I would be too. And that they would find me giddy at the idea that what I thought was going to be a casual fun celebration of our engagement had *two minutes ago, turned into our wedding!* Unfortunately, their arrival was inconveniently timed with my meltdown.

I was still processing everything and they were all ready for the party to begin. I wasn't thrilled with the bouquet of lilies Adam had given me with the letter. Since this was going to be an outdoor wedding, I wondered if they could be exchanged for something more casual, like daisies. When my mom showed me the loose-fitting, jersey, pastel bridesmaid dresses they had chosen, my eyes widened. Those had to go! But was there time to find different dresses? Adam and I both had wanted to have our parents' and grandparents' wedding photos on display at the reception. Were they there? Adam assured me they were and that we had plenty of time to change anything I wanted to change.

Did all of my bridesmaids know? Were they going to be here? The thought of Elyse not being in my wedding caused a new wave of tears. Elyse had just started a new job out of town as a wedding planner, and I knew she was scheduled to be at a wedding that day. She was planning on showing up for the engagement party later that evening, but she'd already warned me she would be late. I called her, and we exchanged a series of OMG statements:

"Can you believe this is happening?"

"I'm so excited for you. But you better believe that Adam's gonna hear a few words from me for not telling me!"

"I know he's just so romantic, he wanted it to be a big secret."

"It *is* soooooo romantic. Of course I'll be there!"

"You'd better because I'm not doing this without you."

We hung up, and she went to tell her brand new boss that she was leaving because her best friend's crazy romantic fiancé planned a surprise wedding and well, she had to be in it.

During my crying meltdown, Adam started to panic. Had he

made a bad call on how I would handle all of this? Did his romantic side finally get the better of him? Was I going to bolt and leave him a *Dear Adam* letter? Adam's sister Shannon swooped in and saved the day. She took us aside, away from all of the excitement, and reminded me that Adam knew exactly what kind of wedding I wanted. We had been planning it on Pinterest for the past six months and talked about it in our letters. The top five things I really cared about, that I had been saying all along were the most important parts of the wedding, were:

1. ~~That I have great hair.~~   *1. That I marry Adam.*
2. ~~That I marry Adam.~~   *2. That I have great hair.*
3. That we document it with a photographer and videographer.
4. That we have good music.
5. That we dance the night away and everyone has SO much fun.

She was right. I was focusing on bridesmaid dresses and flowers and there in front of me was the man I loved, who had spent months pulling together the perfect surprise. I trusted Adam. I knew that he had it covered. I kissed him and thanked him for everything he had done to make this day so special. Adam let out a big sigh of relief.

After all the drama, the poor guy needed some air. He went for a motorcycle ride with his brother Brad, brother-in-law James, dad, and grandpa. Someone handed me a mimosa. I sipped it while the hairdresser Melissa got started on my wedding hair, and by the time my glass was empty, I was good. This *was* fun and exciting. I was the luckiest girl in the world.

How many women have a wedding without all the stress and aggravation and Bridezilla moments mixed in? Well okay, I'd just had a *few* Bridezilla moments myself, but given the circumstances those were understandable. My bridesmaids Jess, Sulienne, Shannon, and Melissa were great. In bridesmaid fashion, they jumped in to do whatever needed to be done. We started with the bridesmaid dresses. Sulienne had been searching dress stores for an hour, sending me pictures to my phone, but nothing she sent looked right. Finding one dress in everyone's size at the last minute that we all liked wasn't going to happen. So, we decided to go with simple black. All the girls already had black dresses they liked. Even my photographer pitched in by going out and buying me a pretty white bra and underwear because I hadn't had time to shop for wedding undies, since I didn't realize I would be needing them quite so soon.

Once I calmed down, everything came together. I wore my mom's earrings, the pearl bracelet I found for 2 pounds at a British charity shop, and Sulienne picked up flip flops for all of us to wear while she was out hunting for dresses – white for me, black for the bridesmaids. By my second mimosa, I realized everything was perfect and that all that really mattered was that I was marrying the man of my dreams.

When Elyse raced through the door a few hours later, the hairdresser and makeup artist were ready to erase some of the frenzy and panic the day had caused her. As soon as she was ready to go, we loaded into cars and headed to Adam's uncle's house for the big event.

Little did I know the drama wasn't quite over. When Adam was on the way to the wedding on his motorcycle, he thought he dropped his phone. When he pulled off the road to turn around and look for it, his dad thought he was having second thoughts or cold feet. To be honest, his parents thought he was pretty crazy for planning the whole surprise wedding in the first place, but in the end they trusted Adam and they believed that he knew me and loved me. But when his dad saw him flip his motorcycle around, for a brief minute he wondered if all the earlier stress had caused Adam to have doubts. Thankfully, he was proven wrong when Adam rounded the corner holding up his phone smiling.

Adam's Uncle Tony and Aunt Joey had graciously agreed to host the decoy engagement party. They were not in on the secret, but started to get suspicious when the decorating began. They had a beautiful property that backed onto an endless grove of apple trees. It had been the backdrop for many parties, and Uncle Tony was the ultimate host. It was a perfect venue.

Adam had been busy all week setting up for the wedding. Now I got why he'd been "working" so much my first week home. He'd arranged wooden picnic tables for the reception under tents, and the band was set up under the awning by the pool.

As guests began to arrive, they started to suspect something was up. Sipping on champagne, they murmured, "What do you think the arbor decorated with flowers is for?"

"I don't know, but the way those chairs are lined in front of it, it looks like a wedding."

"You think?"

Adam knew if he was going to pull off a surprise wedding, he could only trust a handful of people with his secret. My parents knew what he was planning. My mom had known when we were shopping for wedding dresses in London. And a few members of his family knew. All of them had somehow managed to keep his secret. He hadn't told Elyse or the other bridesmaids because he was worried I would eventually find out.

A few guests couldn't make it and because they thought it was just an engagement party, they didn't shuffle their schedules to be there. A few showed up late and were stunned to see me in a wedding dress. My poor university roommate Sarah missed the whole ceremony because she got lost on the back roads and I obviously wasn't checking my phone to give her directions because I *was getting married*!!! But most of the people we both wanted to be there, Adam either told them his secret or strongly encouraged them to be there no matter what.

Most people didn't put two-and-two together until Katie, our MC for the evening, took the microphone and began to read a very special letter, the letter that I had read just a few hours earlier. She invited everyone to make their way to the chairs. It didn't sink in for some that it was a wedding and not an engagement party until

Shannon, Adam's sister and the officiant for the wedding, took her place under the arbor or until Adam made a grand motorcycle entrance and joined her there.

Both my parents walked me down the aisle. And the minute I saw all my friends and family, all the people I loved gathered together in that special place for our special day, I sobbed.

Shannon summed up the day perfectly in her speech. She said, "Carly, I've got to tell you that many months ago, when Adam phoned and let me in on this little secret, several different thoughts went through my mind. And I'm sure you can relate, particularly after a morning like you've had. I thought, *What will Carly think? This is so Adam, he's always been a true romantic. What will Carly think? How will he pull it all off? This is crazy.* But in the end, I thought, *This is perfect!* And now here we are, and I am so blessed to stand here with you as the two of you have chosen to say yes to love."

CHAPTER 27

RE-ENTRY

R e-entry back into "the real world" was a bit of a blur. My life had completely shifted. It took about two months to feel fully landed and like I could breathe a normal pace without my heart or stomach doing flip-flops. The thing that was most hard to fathom or explain was the feelings of overwhelm when there was simply so much to be grateful for. So much joy, so much happiness, so many good things that didn't logically add up to overwhelm. Turns out so much joy can sometimes be hard to swallow, too.

The truth was, a lot had happened in those two months. I was reunited with my love, busy seeing friends and family, being welcomed home by the local media, then a surprise wedding. A. WEDDING. The wedding itself lifted me up on a hot air balloon and launched me so high in the sky that I felt like I was screaming down to anyone in earshot how in love and happy I was, how amazing and incredible and beautiful life was and just how full of joy I was.

A road trip honeymoon with Katie and Matt to the East Coast of Canada swept me off my feet like I was on *The Bachelor*. I was finally with the man I loved, experiencing the cream of the crop and batting

Honeymoon in Halifax

my eyes at the romance of travelling with my new husband after flying solo in England for so long. When we returned home from our honeymoon after quite a bit of time off social media, I found it interesting to even go online. It had been like a companion to me while I was away, and I started to question my relationship with it. In a way, our honeymoon felt like a social media detox.

We then returned home to figure out a place to live. The next few weeks consisted of going to look at homes for sale in the hometown I hadn't lived in for well over 10 years, which gave me heart palpitations that I'm sure made our real estate agent want to run for the hills. We moved back into my parents' house into the room that I outgrew at 17 and then decided to move into my in-laws' basement. I was called back to work early and tried with all of my strength to not compare my new two-hour commute to my former two-minute drive from my beloved apartment just down the river from work.

At work, I was welcomed back so warmly it brought tears to my eyes. My co-workers were some of my biggest supporters over the past year. My customers were so happy to see me and wanted to hear all about my journey between transactions. It was beautiful to be back. Beautiful, but different. Everything. Felt. Different. Naturally, my writing went on the backburner.

It wasn't long until we found a more permanent place to live. We decided to rent for a little while and settled on a cute little 1970s home by the lake. The moment that we signed the lease we both felt a bit of weight lift because of having a place sorted. Finally, we had a place to be us, to be married and to land. It was a place to figure out where we wanted to be, and to finally start our lives as husband and wife.

Just as we were getting ourselves settled, our fairytale ending to a fairytale journey wasn't done surprising us. The short video our videographer made of our wedding he had posted on his website went viral. You may have seen it – Carly and Adam's Surprise Wedding.

That was when the calls started coming in. The most shocking of the bunch was "Good Morning America". They called while I was at work. I still remember the feeling of walking over to my boss' desk asking (but more telling) if they'd survive without me for the day. I had to go get my hair done. My brother even called me to tell me that Steve Harvey was on the "Today Show" talking about the crazy guy who surprised his fiancé with a wedding. We had a CTV interview the next morning, along with an Australian morning show that sent us to a downtown Detroit satellite studio that evening. We made a night of it and cheersed at an expensive seafood restaurant nearby. We surely wouldn't have a day like this again in our lives. It was all quite the rush.

Going viral on the Australian Morning Show

CHAPTER 28

MOVING WEST

T he snow started to fall and Adam's roofing season came to an end. It wasn't long until he started expressing interest in using his teaching degree more than a few supply teaching calls a month. After weighing out options between going abroad to teach or moving elsewhere in Canada, we decided to make the move west. I wasn't very surprised that our lives were leading us there, and it felt refreshing that we were getting ourselves ready for another adventure, one that would inevitably have us saying goodbye to our family, friends, and all that we knew, just as my grandmother did decades earlier.

Seasons passed and the time eventually came to pack our lives into boxes and begin our drive across the country. As we packed our final things into the car that day and took one last walk through the house, we hugged side by side and took in the sight of the empty space. In that moment, I felt full. I was filled to the brim with gratitude and nostalgia and felt that familiar wave of bitter-sweetness that happens with these kinds of moves. Gone were the days of the gorgeous lake sunsets or the echoing voice of the final boarding call for the ferry. That cute little house with a view held us through our first year of marriage. We moved in the fall – my favourite season of the year. We endured the longest winter since the 70s and enjoyed its brilliance turning from the sweetness of spring to the warmth of summer.

I have always had a tendency to fall in love with places, and this one took the cake. Not that it was better than the house that I grew up in or my very own apartment in the city – it was just that I had my new husband with me for this one. There were we's and ours plastered on the walls that made this place different. It made this place home.

As we made our way west, we stopped for ball games in the states, jammed to tunes through the prairies, and were left speechless with the first glimpse of the Rockies. In a way, it felt like the finale to the retrace of my grandmother's footsteps. Together with my husband, we walked hand in hand toward our new life together, leaving all we knew behind.

Months later on a random Tuesday in April in our new little home in BC, I was doing dishes after a lovely meal made by Adam. He came up behind me and kissed me on the shoulder. It was a simple moment, but it hit me like a wave. This right here was what I desperately wanted while I was in England, to be in his presence and to share a life with him. I was exactly where I wanted to be.

WHEN JOURNEYS COLLIDE

After arriving in Canada and reuniting with my grandfather, my grandparents led a rich and layered life. My grandmother joined clubs and organizations, they made friends and travelled, they had children and then grandchildren. She danced and sang and brought joy to the people around her. She embraced life and opportunities and never looked back.

Dear Grama,

I was on a mission that day that not even the rain could disrupt. As I made my way to Westminster Bridge to recreate this photo of you, I remember thinking about the beauty of perspective. Not only was I grateful to have found this photograph of you in front of this very spot decades earlier, but to be there giggling to myself as the wind blew my umbrella inside out, left me in awe. How did I get here? Who's crazy idea was this? I actually made this happen?

Looking back at this photo now, eight years later, it makes me realize that anything is possible. The incredibly unpredictable journeys that brought you to this bridge, then brought me to this bridge, then gave me the urge to dig up this photograph to have another look are more connected than I ever knew possible. The layers and years in constant dance with one another creating beauty and rhythm with every step.

Well, Grama, I did it. I am finally holding my book in these tiny little hands of mine. The book that is laced with both of our fingerprints, decades apart. The book that I get to wrap a beautiful red ribbon around for each of my children, because since day one, this has been for them. Our stories will live on, Grams. Not only through this book, but through the lineage that was created by the life decisions you made in the 40s and the decisions that I am making with my life now.

I didn't do this alone, Grama. I couldn't have done this without you. I hope it makes you proud.

With a granddaughter's love & admiration,
Carly xoxo

ACKNOWLEDGEMENTS

As most people in my life are aware, I have been working on this book on and off for eight years. So many important things have happened in between: moving across the country, buying our first home, starting our family, and starting new careers. I did a lot of work on this beautiful book in the years of 2013 – 2016 with key people that I'm so thrilled to thank right now.

Thank you to my Papa for giving me his blessing when I came up with the idea in 2012. Thank you to Marty Gervais and the Ontario Arts Council for the inspiration and writing grant. Thank you to Linda Sivertsen for starting the Beautiful Writers Group that connected me with fellow writers and led to incredible life experiences with my writing journey. Thank you to Steph Jagger, Patti M. Hall, Jen Hanover, and Sarah Woods for reading my early pages, always encouraging me and for being on this writing journey with me. A huge thank you to Sandra O'Donnell for the hours and hours we spent with coffee and Post-Its and Grama's letters polishing this story into what it is today. I would not have made it this far without your help.

To my cheerleaders since day one...and there are too many to list, but here goes: Jess, Elyse, Lisa, Dawn, Katie, Matt, Sarah, Sharon, Ryan, Sulienne, Cindy, Carla, and of course Mary the Fairy. To my friends and family and co-workers and all of the amazingly supportive people I've met along the way. Thank you to all of the "characters" in this book. The journey wouldn't have been what it was without our paths crossing and for that I am grateful.

Thank you to The Reach Gallery in Abbotsford, BC for featuring my installation piece of all 110 love letters. It was a dream come true for me.

Thank you to Lindsey Smith and Alexandra Franzen and the team at YouCanGetItDone.com who helped me see this book to completion.

Thank you to my Dad for giving me the creative gene and inspiration since I was little and for always being in my corner.

Thank you to my Mom for, gosh, everything. Since the day you gave birth to me, you have been my #1 fan and have scraped me off the floor too many times to count. Thank you for always believing in me and for being there for me always and forever.

Thank you to Adam for being exactly who you are. You have supported this dream since the moment we met, and I cannot thank you enough. I love you so much.

Throughout the years this book often got lovingly put to the side, especially those early years with the kids. While on maternity leave during the pandemic of 2020 when we were all home together, I decided that this was the time. In the summer months especially, Adam would take the boys for walks to the park in the mornings and I would have a few solid hours to dive in. That was when my oldest son Jude started to really understand that his mommy was writing a book. He was always so sweet and encouraging and would come home from the park and ask me how it went. Just this week he asked more questions about it than he ever has before.

"Mommy, when you're done the book can I have my own copy?" he asked.

"Of course, buddy." I said.

"What is the book about?" he asked

"It's about 110 love letters that Nana's Mom and Dad wrote, your Great Grama and Great Papa. Their names were Rene and Nick. And it's about Mommy and Daddy and how we fell in love and wrote letters too," I explained

He then went on to ask, "Are there going to be any pictures in your book? Are there going to be any pictures of *me*? Are there any letters to me?"

Truthfully, this entire book is for you, sweet boy. And it has been since before you were born. This book is for you, Jude, and your little brother Maddox and the sweet little baby that's growing in my belly as I write this. And for all of your children and your children's children.

May the life stories of our family continue to live on with as much love as I feel for you. Today and always, my child. It's all for you. Mama loves you. Xox

ABOUT THE AUTHOR

C arly Butler Verheyen is a writer, photographer, and administrative assistant. What began as a journey of retracing the steps of her grandmother in 2013 turned into a blog, a book, and calling. She has been invited to speak about the legacy of letters and the wisdom of past generations to university students, historical organizations, and genealogy groups. Her story has been featured in media outlets such as *BBC Breakfast, The Times, London's Evening Standard, BuzzFeed, Huffington Post,* "Today Show", "Good Morning America", *the Global News,* and more. Currently, she lives in British Columbia, Canada with her husband Adam and children.

CPSIA information can be obtained
at www.ICGtesting.com
Printed in the USA
BVHW041656201021
619448BV00009B/69